GW00645364

Research Center Books of Related Interest
Ask your bookseller for the books you have missed

ENTRANCE TO THE ZOHAR, compiled and edited by Dr. Philip S. Berg

ENTRANCE TO THE TREE OF LIFE, compiled and edited by Dr. Philip S. Berg

REINCARNATION: THE WHEELS OF A SOUL, by Dr. Philip S. Berg (also edited in Hebrew, Spanish and French)

KABBALAH FOR THE LAYMAN I, by Dr. Philip S. Berg (also edited in Hebrew, Spanish, French, Russian and German)

KABBALAH FOR THE LAYMAN II, by Dr. Philip S. Berg

KABBALAH FOR THE LAYMAN III, by Dr. Philip S. Berg

TEN LUMINOUS EMANATIONS, vol. 1, compiled and edited by R. Levi Krakovsky

TEN LUMINOUS EMANATIONS, vol. 2, compiled and edited by Dr. Philip S. Berg

LIGHT OF REDEMPTION, by R. Levi Krakovsky

GENERAL PRINCIPLES OF KABBALAH, by R.M. Luzatto

THE KABBALAH CONNECTION, by Dr. Philip S. Berg

ASTROLOGY, THE STAR CONNECTION, by Dr. Philip S. Berg

ZOHAR: PARASHAT PINHAS, vols. 1, 2 and 3 translated and edited by Dr. Philip Berg

POWER OF THE ALEPH BETH, vols. 1 and 2 by Dr. Philip S. Berg

KABBALISTIC MEDITATION, by Dr. Philip S. Berg (in cassete tapes)

KABBALAH FOR BEGINNERS, by Karen Berg(in cassete tapes)

THE ZOHAR:

PARASHAT PINHAS

THE

Volume III

RESEARCH CENTER OF KABBALAH PRESS
JERUSALEM — NEW YORK

ZOHAR
PARASHAT PINHAS

Translated and edited

by

DR. PHILIP S. BERG

Copyright © 1988 by Philip S.Berg
All rights reserved

NO PART OF THIS PUBLICATION MAY BE REPRODUCED OR
TRANSMITTED IN ANY FORM OR BY ANY MEANS, ELECTRONIC OR
MECHANICAL, INCLUDING PHOTOCOPY, RECORDING, OR ANY
INFORMATION STORAGE AND RETRIEVAL SYSTEM, WITHOUT
PERMISSION IN WRITING FROM THE PUBLISHER, EXCEPT BY A
REVIEWER WHO WISHES TO QUOTE BRIEF PASSAGES IN
CONNECTION WITH A REVIEW WRITTEN FOR INCLUSION IN A
MAGAZINE, NEWSPAPER OR BROADCAST.

FIRST EDITION
June 1988

ISBN 0-943688-54-X (Hardcover)
0-943688-55-8 (Softcover)

For further information, address:
RESEARCH CENTRE OF KABBALAH
200 PARK AVENUE, SUITE 303E
NEW YORK, N.Y. 10017
—OR—
RESEARCH CENTRE OF KABBALAH
P.O.BOX 14168
THE OLD CITY, JERUSALEM
ISRAEL

PRINTED IN U.S.A.

THE PUBLICATION OF THIS VOLUME

HAS BEEN MADE POSSIBLE THROUGH

THE GENEROUS SUPPORT OF

SYLVIA DWECK

DEDICATED TO THOSE KABBALISTS WHO

ARE TRYING TO PULL TOGETHER

DIVERSE ASPECTS OF NATURE INTO

ONE NEW, MEANINGFUL WHOLE...

TABLE OF CONTENTS

MINGLED WITH BEATEN OIL
(661) *Beaten Oil* (662) *Yesod and the Righteous* (Commentary) *Oil and Upper Hokhmah*

THE FAITHFUL SHEPHERD
(663) *Oil Beaten as Biblical Precepts* (664) *Upper Hokhmah* (665) *Three Intellects* (666) *Lower Chariots* (667) *Burnt offerings*

THE FAITHFUL SHEPHERD
(668) *Fourth Sephirah* (Commentary) *Three Beasts* (669) *Divine Throne* (Commentary) *Malkhut*

THE FAITHFUL SHEPHERD
(670) *Six Sephirot* (671) *New Moons and their Heads* (Commentary) *The Attire of Ze'ir Anpin* (672) *Two Young Bullocks* (673) *Descent in a Sin Offering* (674) *Hokhmah and Hasadim are drawn from the Chest* (675) *The Upper Three and the Lower Seven* (Commentary) *Inclusiveness of the Sefirot* (676) *Jacob and Joseph as Ze'ir Anpin* (677) *Two Kings and One Crown*

THE FAITHFUL SHEPHERD
(678) *One Year Old Lamb* (Commentary) *Sefirot of the Moon* (679) *Contractions of the Moon* (680) *How to Avoid Enemies* (681) *Goat as Azazel* (682) *Keter and Its Three Stages* (683) *Suckling in Malkhut*

THE FAITHFUL SHEPHERD
(684) *Generations of Joseph and Jacob* (685) *Woman and the Evil Forces* (686) *Six Directions of the Moon* (687) *Points of Energy from the Moon* (688) *Why is Malkhut Called Moon* (Commentary) *Right side and Hasadim* (689) *Knowledge of Good and Evil* (690) *The Tree of Life* (Commentary) *Illuminations of Netsach and Hod of Ze'ir Anpin*

THE FAITHFUL SHEPHERD
(733) *The Tongue as a Rod* (734) *The Best of Egypt* (735)
Future Punishment (736) *Judgement by Roasting Fire* (737)
Seven Days No Leaven (738) *Matsah and the Planets* (739)
Guarding the Hidden Yod

REBUKE THE WILD BEAST OF THE REEDS
(740) *What is the Reed* (Commentary) *Lillith and Samael* (741)
Secret of Chamets (742) *The Broken foot of the Reed*
(Commentary) Malkhut in Relation to Chamets

THE FAITHFUL SHEPHERD
(743) *Gabriel and the Reed* (744) *First and Second Temple* (745)
The Gall of the Calf and Healing (Commentary) *Wild Beast
and the Romans* (746) *Chet and Hey*

FOUR REDEMPTIONS
(747) *The Souls Belonging to Jacob* (748) *The Four Cups of
Wine* (749) *Four Celestial Beings* (750) *72 Names*

BIRD"S NEST
(751) *Young Ones or Eggs* (752) *Kabbalists Come from the
Aleph* (753) *Ascension to the Central Column*

THE FOUR SECTIONS IN THE PHYLACTERIES OF THE
RECITAL OF THE SHEMA ISRAEL
(754) *Numerical Value of One* (755) *The King's Banquet*

THE SHEW-BREAD THAT HAS 12 COUNTENANCES
(756) *The Food of the Offering* (Commentary) *Celestial Beings*
(757) *12 Countenances* (Commentary) *Malkhut and the King's
Table* (758) *The Oven as the Sekhinah* (759) *Clean Pure Flour*
(760) *Fire of the Most High*

THE FAITHFUL SHEPHERD
A BIRD'S NEST

MOSE'S BRIDE

YOU SHALL PRESENT AN OFFERING MADE
BY FIRE, A BURNT OFFERING

AND IN THE DAY OF THE FIRST-FRUITS

THE DAY OF ATONEMENT

THE FESTIVAL OF BOOTHS

TEN THINGS THAT A MAN MUST OBSERVE AT THE SABBATH TABLE (Continuation)

636) And the sixth correction is that he should not be a voracious glutton at the King's table, as was Esau, who said: "Let me swallow" (Genesis 25:30), gulping it down, but by way of mastication, chewing the food with his teeth. So, too, one who produces words of prayer or words of Torah from his mouth, should bring them out, chewed over, and complete; i.e. he should consider them and go over them, as though chewing them over, and not in a gulping fashion and incomplete. And futhermore, because of the danger that the food might enter his trachea instead of his oesophagus, he must eat by way of masticating and not gulping.

637) And the seventh correction is water at the end of the meal, as it has been taught: Water to wash the hands at the beginning of the meal is a precept and at the end of the meal is an obligation, while in the middle (between courses) it is optional. (Cf. Talmud Bavli, Hullin, 105a.) With the water at the beginning of the meal, he has to raise his fingers up so that the dirty water will not run back and defile the hands. (Cf. Talmud Bavli, Sotah 4b.) And there are sages who held the opinion that the water at the end of the meal is because of Sodom salt, lest it blind the eyes (Cf. Talmud Bavli, Hullin, 105b.)

They thereby removed from us the obligation, for to wash the hands at the end of the meal is no more than good advice, and not obligatory. And there are secret matters with those who held that water to wash the hands at the end of the meal is obligatory. And it is not good practice to contradict the words of the great, but to them may be applied the verse: "According to the law which they shall teach you" (Deuteronomy 17:11).

638) And futhermore, three sanctifications were stated in this connection, as it is written: "Sanctify yourselves therefore, and be holy; for I am holy" (Leviticus 11:44). "Sanctify yourselves" refers to the water for washing the hands at the beginning of the meal. "And be holy" refers to the water at the end of the meal. "For... holy" is palatable [Hebrew root: ayyin resh beit] oil to remove the filth from the fingers. "I am the Lord" is a blessing. And the water in the middle is between cheese and meat, and this is why it is written: "Sanctify yourselves therefore and be holy, for I (the Lord) am holy" (ibid.). Happy is this people whose master places them near to Him, and who infects them with his holiness!

639) So, too, "Sanctify yourselves" (Leviticus 11:44) refers to the time of sexual intercourse. The initial emission of a man's seed is a precept, i.e. keeping of the commandment to be fruitful and multiply (see Genesis 1:28), while the latter is the seed of the female, which is obligatory, that is to say: the seed of the male obligates her to produce seed. And that in the middle is hinted at in "and curdled me like cheese" (Job 10:10), i.e. the Holy One, blessed be He, who gives solid form to the seed for the building up of the embryo, as it is written: "Have You not poured me out like milk, and curdled me like cheese?" (ibid.). And this is the allusion to the waters that are in the middle, between cheese and meat (see 638), for it is said about Him, about the Holy One, blessed be He: "You have clothed me with skin and flesh" (ibid. v.11).

COMMENTARY:

The meaning of cheese is building up, since cheese is a solidification of milk which is liquid. Meat refers to the Holy One, blessed be He, who turns the seed into flesh, this being the secret of the water in the middle. That is to say: The water of the Holy One, blessed be He, is in the middle, between the Male Waters of the male and the Female Waters of the female.

640) The eighth correction is that at least three persons must be present for the cup of benediction. Why? Because the cup alludes to Binah, and Binah is the third of the ten Sephirot, when counting them from the top downwards, i.e. Keter-Hokhmah-Binah. For this reason, if less than three persons are present, the cup is not required. Another explanation of the ruling that at least three persons must be present for the cup of benediction is that it refers to "They call You thrice holy" [The third benediction in the reader's repetition of the shemoneh esreh in the Additional Service of the Sabbath, Sephardi, not Ashkenazi version — tr.]. Furthermore, the Torah did not descend less than three, namely: Priests, Levities, and Israelites (the three divisions of the Hebrew Bible) Torah, Prophets, and Hagiographa, and it was given in the third month, on the third day. And this Binah is the first three letters, yod hey waw, of the Tetragrammaton [yod hey waw and hey], which is the secret of the three columns. And in its regard they said: The night has three watches. (Cf. Talmud Bavli, Berakhot 3a.) And Malkhut is hey, the fourth letter of the Tetragrammaton [yod hey waw and hey] and receives all three of the columns, and about it they said: The night has four watches (ibid.), corresponding to the three columns and Malkhut that receives them. And the letter shin,

with the three arms, corresponds to the three watches, while the letter shin, with four arms, corresponds to the four watches.

641) And the ninth correction is the cup of benediction, that is one-quarter of a log [a liquid measure — tr.], the amount corresponding to the letter hey, which is the fourth letter of the Tetragrammaton [yod hey waw and hey]. And the tenth correction is that when there are ten people present, he who says grace adds 'our God' (Mishnah, Berakhot 7, 3). The reason for this is that the lower Shekhinah, which is Malkhut, is both fourth and tenth — the fourth letter of the Tetragrammaton and the tenth in the count of the Sephirot, which are the secret of the ten letters yod waw dalet, hey aleph, waw aleph waw, hey aleph, [these being the four letters of the Tetragrammaton spelled out and filled in with alephs — tr.], and therefore the presence of ten persons is required in order to mention the name 'our God.' And a man must be very careful not to throw these matters in a place where he shouldn't, like one who throws away bread, and how much more so one who throws out from his table the bread of the Torah, for his table is the Shekhinah, about which it is said: "This is the table that is before the Lord" (Ezekiel 41:22).

THERE ARE THREE WHO HARM THEMSELVES

642) And in the first part, he says: There are three who harm themselves, two of whom are in this world, and one in another world. And these are: The one who curses himself, as we have learnt; one official is appointed before man, and when a man curses himself this official, together with his seventy subordinates, take that word, and respond 'amen,' and they raise it up on high and judge it. And the official follows him

until he does something and then he puts into effect for him the curse of that word that he uttered.

643) Who do we have that is greater than Moses, who said: "And if not, blot me, I pray You, out of Your book which You have written" (Exodus 32:32). This he said for the sake of Israel, and although the Holy One, blessed be He, did what he (Moses) requested and forgave Israel, nevertheless he was not spared punishment, for it has already been noted that his (Moses') name is not mentioned in the Parasha: Tetsaveh (Exodus 27:20, 30:10), but has been blotted out from there. And this has already been taught. And who do we have that is greater than King David, who said: "I said: I will take heed to my ways, that I sin not with my tongue; I will keep a curb on my mouth, while the wicked is before me." (Psalms 39:2). What is the meaning of "while the wicked is before me"? This refers to that official who was appointed over the one who curses himself and who takes that word to harm a man, as above.

644) And one who does harm to himself is the person who throws bread, or crumbs of bread, onto the ground, having no respect for it, as we have learnt (see above, in the Introduction to the Sepher ha-Zohar, 254). And these are the two who receive their punishment in this world. And the one who does harm to himself and receives his punishment in another world is the person who kindles a light towards the end of the Sabbath [during the passages that are recited between the end of the weekday evening service and the Havdalah ceremony with which the Sabbath formally terminates — tr.]. And such a one is considered as a profaner of the Sabbath because he causes the fire of Gehenna (Hell) to be kindled before its time.

645) There is a special place in Gehenna for those who profane the Sabbath. And since he kindles the light before its

time, a certain official exists in Gehenna on Saturday evenings, and he first lights that place and says: This spot is for so-and-so. And all the wicked ones who are in Gehenna help him to heat up that spot, and that official calls out, saying: "Behold, the Lord will hurl you up and down with a man's throw; He will wind you round and round" (Isaiah 22:17). And the wicked who are in Gehenna respond: "He will violently roll and toss you like a ball into a large country; there shall you die" (ibid. v.18). And this is because he caused them to be kindled before time — and this makes three who cause harm to themselves, as we have learnt.

THE FAITHFUL SHEPHERD

THREE YODS IN THE TETRAGRAMMATON FILLED IN WITH YOD MAKE 63

646) Another explanation: "And he dreamed and behold, a ladder" (Genesis 28:12). Faithful Shepherd, just as the letter lamed ascends higher than all the other letters, because the lamed alludes to Binah, so will you in the future be exalted above all creatures. Because you ascended there, to the Tetragrammaton [yod hey waw and hey], filled in with yods, whose numerical value is yod = yod waw dalet, 10 + 6 + 4 = 20; hey = hey yod, 5 + 10 = 15; waw = waw aleph waw, 6 + 1 + 6 = 13; hey = hey yod, 5 + 10 = 1; and: 20 + 15 + 13 + 15 = 63, which is Binah. And the Tetragrammaton filled in with yods there are three yods, the numerical value of each of which is 10, making 30, which is the numerical value of the letter lamed. For initially you were in the Tetragrammaton filled in with alephs [yod = yod waw dalet, 10 + 6 + 4 = 20; hey = hey aleph, 5 + 1 = 6; waw = waw aleph waw, 6 + 1 + 6 = 13; and, hey = hey aleph, 5 + 1 = 6; and 20 + 6 + 13 + 6 = 45],

which is Ze'ir Anpin, and which contains yod aleph aleph
aleph, the numerical value of which is (10 + 1 + 1 + 1)
thirteen, which stands for the thirteen attributes of Mercy (see
Exodus 34:6-8), and has the same numerical value as the word
One [echad: aleph chet dalet, 1 + 8 + 4 = 13], and now you
have ascended to El (God), which is yod yod aleph yod (i.e. the
filling of the Tetragrammaton with yods), whose numerical
value is 63. And both of these Names are witnesses, "Has not
one God created us?" (Malakhi 11:10). For the yod-filling of
the Tetragrammaton [yod yod aleph yod] is the numerical value
of the word God [El], and the aleph-filling of the
Tetragrammaton [yod aleph aleph aleph] is the numerical value
of the word one [echad], which is as is written: "Have we not
all one father? Has not one God created us?" (Malakhi 2:10).

647) And with these three yods of the 63-letter Name [i.e. the
Tetragrammaton filled in with yods — tr.], may the verse be
established in you: "He shall be exalted, and lifted up, and shall
be very high" (Isaiah 52:13). "Very high" [gavah me'od] refers to
the Tetragrammaton filled in with alephs, whose numerical
value is 45 [yod = yod waw dalet, 10 + 6 + 4 = 20; hey = hey
aleph, 5 + 1 = 6; waw = waw aleph waw, 6 + 1 + 6 = 13; and,
hey = hey aleph, 5 + 1 = 6; 20 + 6 + 13 + 6 = 45], which is the
numerical value of the word 'very' [me'od: mem aleph dalet, 40
+ 1 + 4 = 45], which is the same as 'man' [adam: aleph dalet
mem, 1 + 4 + 40 = 45], and in fact the letters of the word
'very' are the same as those of the word 'man', written in
reverse order. "He shall be exalted" [yarum] is the four faces
of the lion, which is Hesed that rises to Hokhmah, which is the
secret of "The Lord will bless you" (Numbers 6:24 — the
priestly benediction), this being the secret of the 72 — letter
Name, that is the Tetragrammaton [yod hey waw and hey]
filled in entirely with yods. Thus: yod = yod waw dalet, 10 + 6
+ 4 = 20; hey = hey yod, 5 + 10 = 15; waw = waw yod waw,

6 + 10 + 6 = 22; hey = hey yod, 5 + 10 = 15; and 20 + 15 + 22
+ 15 = 72], which is the numerical value of Hesed [chet samekh
dalet, 8 + 60 + 4 = 72], and this is Hokhmah of the right. "And
lifted up" [v'nisa'] is the four faces of ox, which is Gevurah
that rises to Binah, namely: "The Lord lift up" (Numbers 6:26),
and this is Binah of the left. "Very high" [gavah me'od] is "The
Lord will make to shine" (Numbers 6:25), which is Ze'ir Anpin,
and is in the middle [i.e. the second of the three verses of the
priestly benediction — tr.], and is the 45 — letter Name, i.e. the
Tetragrammaton filled in with alephs. And the 63-letter filling
of the Tetragrammaton, as above, is: "The Lord lift up His
countenance upon you, and give you peace" (Numbers 6:26).
The fourth Tetragrammaton, i.e. that filled with heys [yod =
yod waw dalet, 10 + 6 + 4 = 20; hey = hey hey, 5 + 5 = 10;
waw = waw waw, 6 + 6 = 12; and, hey = hey hey, 5 + 5 = 10;
and 20 + 10 + 12 + 10 = 52] is Malkhut, and this is: "So they
shall put My name upon the children of Israel, and I will bless
them" (Numbers 6:27), for Malkhut is called 'name.'

AS A FLAME JOINED TO A BURNING COAL

648) From the right-hand side, Malkhut is called a stone; and
a number of smooth precious stones, i.e. stones that issue water
(see above, Bereshit Aleph, 22), are to be derived from it.
From them issue the waters of the Torah, about which we have
learnt: Rabbi Akiva said to his disciples: When you reach stones
of pure marble, do not say: Water, water, lest you endanger
your souls. (Cf. Talmud Bavli, Hagigah 14b.) The meaning of
this is: Do not say that these waters are of Malkhut, that they
are just ordinary water, i.e. only hasadim, because "He that
speaks falsehood shall not be established before My eyes"
(Psalms 101:7), for these waters that are in Malkhut are Torah;

that is to say that they are drawn down from Ze'ir Anpin, who is called Torah, and is composed of Hokhmah and hasadim together, and is therefore the secret of light and not of water, which teaches about hasadim without Hokhmah, for it is said about it: "And the Torah is light" (Proverbs 6:23). And since this light stems from a spring of water that has never disappointed, for Ze'ir Anpin receives this light from upper Father and Mother whose coupling is forever uninterrupted, and there, with Father and Mother, it is hasadim, it is therefore called water, which is hasadim. However, when the hasadim come to Ze'ir Anpin, they are composed of Hokhmah also, and are called light. And this is the secret of "And the Torah is light" (ibid.).

649) And from the left-hand side, this stone, which is yod, i.e. Malkhut, is called a burning coal, i.e. by virtue of the power of the judgments of the left that burn in it, whence the ten Sephirot are referred to as a flame joined to a burning coal, and it has four hues, i.e. the four letters of the simple Tetragrammaton [yod hey waw and hey], and they are ten, i.e. the ten letters of the Tetragrammaton filled in with alephs: yod waw dalet, hey aleph, waw aleph waw, hey aleph. Together this makes 14 letters, where 14 is the numerical value of the word 'hand' [yad: yod dalet, $10 + 4 = 14$]. And it is the large hand from the point of view of the right which is Hesed, the mighty hand from the point of view of the left which is Gevurah (might), while from the point of view of the central column it is an upraised hand. It is thus composed of 42 hues, this being the sum of three times 14 (= hand).

650) And since from the point of view of the right it is a stone, and from the point of view of the left it is a burning coal, the Holy One, blessed be He, takes vengeance with it from Ishmael and Edom, who are derived from the waste

matters of right and left. For they are strange fires of the evil forces and the malicious waters, where Ishmael is malicious waters and Edom is strange fires, and their officials are Samael and Serpent. Samael, who is the fire of Gehenna (Hell), is appointed over the nation of Esau [i.e. Edom — tr.], and Serpent is appointed over the nation of Ishmael, and this is the angel Rachab, who is in charge of the waters.

651) From the right of Abraham, whose level is Hesed, He takes vengeance on Ishmael and his angel, and from the left of Isaac, whose level is Pachad (Fear), i.e. Gevurah, He takes vengeance on Esau and his angel by means of two Messiahs, one of whom, the Messiah son of David, is from the right, while the other, Messiah son of Joseph, is from the left. And the level of Jacob, which is Tipheret, is the central column, that corresponds to them, in the secret of "He (Jacob) guided his hands wittingly" (Genesis 48:14), the lion, to the left, corresponding to Esau, and the ox to the right, corresponding to Ishmael. And since Judah was banished in Esau, it follows that the right of holiness is with the left of Esau, and indeed in the exile of Ishmael the left of holiness is to be found with the impure right of Ishmael. Accordingly, it follows that the Messiah son of David, which is right, will take vengeance from Esau, while the Messiah son of Joseph, which is left, will take vengeance from Ishmael. "As long as he comes to Shiloh" (Genesis 49:10), which verse is read as meaning: Until Shiloh comes, where the numerical value of Shiloh [shin yod lamed hey, 300 + 10 + 30 + 5 = 345] is the same as that of Moses [Moshe: mem shin hey, 40 + 300 + 5 = 345], who is the Faithful Shepherd. The verse therefore is taken as meaning: Until the Faithful Shepherd comes. And Moses, the Faithful Shepherd, whose level is Tipheret Israel, which is the central column, will take vengeance from the mixed multitude (see Exodus XII, 38), for the mixed multitude is composed of the right and left of

impurity, and so the central column, which is composed of the right and left of holiness, will be avenged on them.

COMMENTARY:

And the reason why Jacob, who is the central column, "guided his hands wittingly (Genesis 49:10) is noted above (Va-era, 34), for prior to the central column becoming decisive, the fire was on the right and the waters on the left. But after the central column became decisive, the fire went to the left and the waters to the right, as is explained there.

652) In these three stages, right, left and center, as above, the priests, Levites, and Israelites will be recalled from the Exile, for they are drawn down from these three columns. And in them, in the three columns, He takes vengeance upon Esau, Ishmael, and the mixed multitude, for just as the mixed multitude is intermixed with Esau and Ishmael, i.e. containing right and left of impurity, so Jacob, who is the central column, is composed of Abraham and Isaac, which are right and left, for he is a mixture of the two of them. And so, too, Shiloh [shin yod lamed hey, 300 + 10 + 30 + 5 = 345], which is Moses [Mosheh: mem shin hey, 40 + 300 + 5 = 345], which is also the central column, as above, is intermixed with Messiah son of David, which is the right side, and with Messiah son of Joseph, which is the left side, and he will be the chain that incorporates and connects the two of them, as the vision that Balaam saw in his prophecy, i.e. "As long as he comes to Shiloh" (Genesis 49:10) [interpreted, see above, 651, as meaning:

Until Moses comes]. For thus the two Messiahs are connected with the Faithful Shepherd, this being the secret of the three patriarchs, i.e. the three columns, as above, in the final exile, and they will thus have the power to win and destroy all the shells that correspond to the three columns of holiness, as above.

COMMENTARY:

Even though the Redemption will be effected by the two Messiahs, the Messiah son of David and the Messiah son of Joseph, it is nevertheless impossible for the Redemption to be complete until the soul [neshamah] of Moses is revealed, for this is the secret of the revelation of all the secrets of the Torah. And then the two Messiahs will be able to gain victory over all the shells that are in the world, and this is what is meant by saying that Moses incorporates the two Messiahs, i.e. the revelation of the soul [neshamah] of Moses includes everything. And this is the inner meaning of the verse: "Until Shiloh comes" [see the interpretation, above, of Genesis 49:10], for the Redemption can not be complete until Moses is revealed together with the two Messiahs.

653) He began by quoting: "None has beheld iniquity in Jacob, neither has one seen perverseness in Israel; The Lord his God is with him, and the shouting of the King is among them" (Numbers 23:21 — from the prophecy of Balaam). And all this is to fulfil the scriptural verse: "But with great compassion will I gather you" (Isaiah 54:7). And that time, the shells that

surround the Shekhinah will be shattered into pieces, and immediately one of the three stones will be revealed. And the three stones are Segol [the Hebrew vowel 'e', shaped like three dots, arranged as the corners of an equilateral triangle], and the one stone is the secret of Malkhut, which is the apex of the Segol [as is explained below, 671, q.v.], and about these three points, it is said: "Now it came to pass in the thirtieth year, in the fourth month, on the fifth day of the month" (Ezekiel 1:1). "Thirtieth" is the secret of the three yods, where each of the three points that make up the Segol is a yod, and the numerical sum of three yods is 30. "In the fourth month" refers to the fourth stone, which is Netsach. "In the fifth day of the month" refers to the fifth stone, which is Hod. Corresponding to them is: "And (David) chose five smooth stones out of the brook" (I Samuel 17:40), these five being the secret of Hesed, Gevurah, Tipheret, Netsach, and Hod, that are taken from Yesod that incorporates all of them, and is called brook. And corresponding to them are the five words: Hear, O-Israel, the-Lord, our-God, the-Lord. (The Shema Israel, from Deuteronomy VI, 4.)

COMMENTARY:

When Malkhut ascends to Binah, and there receives from the left column of Binah, it goes higher than Hesed and Gevurah of Ze'ir Anpin, and then is the apex of the Segol in three dots in the shape of an equilateral triangle, and Malkhut is the apex, with Hesed and Gevurah of Ze'ir Anpin as the two corners, at the base. And when Malkhut receives from the three columns of Ze'ir Anpin, it is then fourth of Hesed, Gevurah and Tipheret of Ze'ir Anpin, i.e. in the aspect of Netsach. And

when Malkhut is beneath Ze'ir Anpin, it is then fifth, i.e. the
aspect of Hod, for there is the end, in the secret of: Mother has
spread as far as Hod.

654) "As I was in the Exile" (Ezekiel 1:1). This is the
Shekhinah, which is called 'I', with which the Holy One,
blessed be He, is One [echad], because Ze'ir Anpin is aleph
chet of echad [aleph chet dalet], and the Shekhinah is dalet of
echad. The waw (as) that is added to the 'I' — for it is written
'As I' — is the river, which is the Righteous One, Life of the
Worlds, i.e. Yesod. And this is to be explained as follows: "And
a river went out of Eden to water the garden" (Genesis 11:10).
What is meant by Eden? This is Binah [beit yod nun hey]. The
river that went out of Binah (Eden) is waw the son of [ben:
beit nun] Yah [yod hey], i.e. Ze'ir Anpin, which is the level of
the Faithful Shepherd. And the Faithful Shepherd, which is
Ze'ir Anpin, issues from upper Mother, which is the secret of
Eden, and spreads throughout the six Sephirot: Hesed, Gevurah,
Tipheret, Netsach, Hod and Yesod, to the Righteous One,
which is Yesod. And from there, from Yesod, it waters the
garden, which is the Shekhinah, and so the waw (as) of 'I'
therefore alludes to Yesod that waters it.

655) "As I was in the Exile by the river Kevar" (Ezekiel 1:1).
What is Kevar [kaph beit resh]? The answer to this is that it is
a mnemonic, where kaph alludes to Keter, beit to Binah, and
resh to Reshit Hokhmah. Keter is on the right side; Hokhmah
is on the left side; Binah is in the center. And they form a
Chariot [rekhev: resh kaph beit, i.e. an anagram of Kevar] on
high for the Prime Cause, the Infinite One. All ten of the
Sephirot are included in the river, which is Ze'ir Anpin, which
spreads as far as the Righteous One, which is Yesod, that is
called All, as it is All — inclusive, containing within it all

the Sephirot, and about it was it said: "The tree grew and was strong... and in it was food for all" (Daniel 4:8-9). Everything depends on it. When Ezekiel saw the Shekhinah amongst the shells, he saw ten Sephirot with it. (See above, 248.)

656) It is written: "Fine flour for a meal offering" (e.g. Numbers 7); that is that this fine flour, which is Malkhut, should be brought before the Supreme King for a meal offering between the two arms; that is to say that it should be composed of the two arms, which are Hesed and Gevurah, the right side and the left side.

THE FAITHFUL SHEPHERD

657) And in the first part, the Faithful Shepherd said: From this, from what the Zohar says about the fine flour for a meal offering being between the two arms, it must be understood that these are hidden matters that have to be explained to the companions. It is said about Abraham and Isaac, who instituted the morning and afternoon prayers (cf. Talmud Bavli, Berakhot 26b): "My hand has laid the foundation of the earth, and My right hand has spread out the heavens" (Isaiah 48:13). "My hand" refers to Isaac, who is the left hand of Ze'ir Anpin, and "My right hand" refers to Abraham, who is the right hand side of Ze'ir Anpin, their levels being Hesed and Pachad, as it is said about them: "The Lord has sworn by His right hand, and by the arm of His strength" (Isaiah 62:8), which are the two arms to the King, which is the Tetragrammaton, i.e. Ze'ir Anpin, the central column. And His fine flour is the lower Shekhinah, i.e. Malkhut, which is His light, that is of Ze'ir Anpin, and is clean fine flour from His sides, i.e. cleaving to His right and left sides, without blemish of darkness, and without any implication of darkness. For such is the

relationship of light to darkness, as clean grain to chaff and straw. Malkhut is therefore termed fine flour when it is without any intimation of darkness.

658) But in the iniquities of Israel, darkness becomes mixed up with the lights. And just as a man threshes the grain and then makes his selection of the wheat from the chaff and straw, like one picking out food from amongst rubbish, so it is with Israel that, when darkness becomes intermingled with them, they have to re-make and correct their spirit. And the secret of the matter is contained in the verse: "The sacrifices of God are a broken spirit; a broken and contrite heart, O God, You will not despise" (Psalms 51:19). For darkness, which is the evil inclination that covers the spirit as the chaff that covers the grain or as the cloud that covers the sun not allowing it to give light, is broken.

659) And in the time of darkness, which is the evil inclination that covers the good inclination, the latter, which is light, is like one who is imprisoned in the prison of the evil inclination. And so, too, when the good inclination is imprisoned in the domain of the evil inclination, the hosts of the good inclination are also imprisoned in the domain of the hosts of the evil inclination. And when a person breaks his spirit in all his limbs before the Lord, what does Scripture say? "Saying to the prisoners: 'Go forth'; to them that are in darkness: 'Show yourselves'" (Isaiah 49:9).

660) But the Shekhinah is pure fine flour, in which darkness and gloom can not become mixed up. And it is as a vine that rejects a graft of another sort, that is not of its type. And this thereby the fine flour dwells between the arms of the King, namely Hesed and Gevurah, "mingled with beaten oil" (Numbers 28:5).

MINGLED WITH BEATEN OIL

661) "Mingled with beaten oil" (Numbers 28:5). With oil refers
to that oil that is poured out and issues from on high, from
Hokhmah of the right side. Rabbi Shimeon said: What you have
said is good, but how do you explain "beaten" of the oil in the
verse? The answer is that it is a divine secret. Since we are
talking about oil, what is the sense of "beaten"? It is an allusion
to the mating with the Female, i.e. Malkhut, to draw down to
her beaten oil as is fitting for her, from upper Hokhmah,
which is none other than beaten in order to extract oil from the
olives, which are the limbs of the body, i.e. the Sephirot of
Ze'ir Anpin, termed body, and to draw that emanation down
from above, from upper Hokhmah, with each and every limb.

662) And the Righteous one, which is Yesod, is the one who
brays with pestles and extracts from all those upper limbs,
from the Sephirot of Ze'ir Anpin, that are holy olives,
annointing oil, with a perfect longing for the Female, which is
Malkhut. But if he does not bray, that oil will issue forth only
without the longing of the limbs, and the Female will have no
enjoyment from that emanation, and the oil, which is the light
of Hokhmah, will not be fitting until it is mixed of all the
limbs. Therefore it is written: "Mingled with beaten oil"
(Numbers 28:5), in order to enjoy it and be nourished from it.

COMMENTARY:

The oil, which is the light of upper Hokhmah that is on the
right, is not fitting until it is composed of all the columns, i.e.
the three columns from the chest and upwards of Ze'ir Anpin,

and the three columns from the chest and downwards of Ze'ir Anpin; and the unity of the columns is achieved only by the curtain of Chireq that is in the central column (as above, Lekh, page 13). And this is the secret of 'beaten,' for the judgments of the curtain of Chireq bray the left column until it joins with the right, and the three columns become united with each other (as is clarified there) And the main subject of the curtain of Chireq of the central column is Yesod, which is at its conclusion. And on the text: "And the Righteous One... is the one who brays" with pestles: i.e. awakens the curtain of Chireq to bray the left column with it. "And extracts from all those upper limbs... that are holy olives": For, by the braying of Yesod, all the limbs that are above the chest of Ze'ir Anpin unite, this being the secret of the three columns Hesed, Gevurah and Tipheret; and all the limbs that are below the chest of Ze'ir Anpin unite this being the secret of the three columns Netsach, Hod, and Yesod; and they all become one and it is drawn down from all of them together. "With a perfect longing for the Female:" For they then draw down the anointing oil, which is the secret of the light of upper Hokhamah, with a great longing towards Malkhut. And on the text: "But if he does not bray, that oil will issue forth only without the longing of the limbs." For if he had not awakened the curtain of Chireq to bray the left column with it, the left would never have united with the right, and the perfect oil would never have come forth by means of the three columns to Malkhut. (As is clarified there.)

THE FAITHFUL SHEPHERD

663) The Faithful Shepherd said to Rabbi Shimeon: Holy Luminary, how sweet are your words! It is certainly said here

(Numbers 28:5) "Mingled with beaten oil," and it says there, in
the Oral Law, that it is beaten in Bible, Mishnah, and Talmud
(Cf. Talmud Bavli, Sanhedrin 24a.) And there is yet a second
secret here in "Mingled with beaten oil." It is certainly not the
Torah that is beaten in Bible, Mishnah, and Talmud, but the
person who suffers a number of chastisements because of it, as
the sages of the Mishnah taught: The Torah is only upheld by
one who kills himself for it. (Cf. Talmud Bavli, Berakhot 63b.)
And they said further: When you trudge from county to county
to learn Torah, you will be privileged to see the face of the
Shekhinah. (Cf. Talmud Bavli, Babba Batra, 8a.)

664) Again: "Mingled with beaten oil (Numbers 28:5)." This
refers to one who keeps the injunction: You shall eat bread
with salt "and you shall drink water by measure (Ezekiel 4:11)
(Mishnah, Pirkey Avoth 6, 4)." Again, "Mingled with beaten
oil" corresponds to "But he was wounded because of our
transgressions, he was crushed of our iniquities (Isaiah 53:5)."
And again, "Mingled with beaten oil" refers to the Righteous
One, Life of the Worlds, which is Yesod, that draws down holy
drops that are olive-like crumbs from the upper brain, which is
upper Hokhmah, which are one-tenth corresponding to yod,
two-tenths to yod yod, and three-tenths to yod yod yod. And
these are: "three-tenths for a bullock and two-tenths for the
ram... and a tenth each for each lamb..." (Numbers 28:20-21).

665) And the secret of the matter is as they said in *Tractate
Taanit*: Not one drop (of rain) descends from above without
two drops (of moisture) coming up to meet it from below. [The
text in Talmud Bavli, Taanit 25b, has 'handbreadth' instead of
'drop,' and 'three' instead of 'two.' A parallel text in Midrash
Bereshit Rabba 13, 13, has 'handbreadth' instead of 'drop,' but
'two,' as our text, not 'three.' — tr.] And they are in this secret:
.˙. . And their allusion corresponds to three intellects: of
memory, of thought, and of imagination. Imagination and

memory ascend from the heart, the thoughts descend to them
to the heart, and the imagination and the memory welcome
them as a king. Because this man, which is thought, mounts
and controls the third being, descending on it to the two beings
that open their wings to receive it, just as a cholem placed over
a tsere becomes a segolta. And this is upper Keter, above
Hokhmah and Binah. [From the beginning of 665 appears to be
a marginal note which the copyists incorporated into the book.]

666) One-tenth and two-tenths allude to the three beings of
the upper Chariot, are called Gedulah, which is Hesed,
Gevurah, and Tipheret. Three-tenths alludes to Netsach, Hod,
and Yesod, in which is the second, lower, Chariot. The fourth
part of a hin [for the drink-offering, see Numbers 28 — tr.] is
holy Malkhut, which is hey, the fourth letter of the
Tetragrammaton [yod hey waw and hey], in which are the four
faces of a man. For in Hesed there are four faces of a lion; in
Gevurah there are four faces of an ox; and in Tipheret there
are four faces of an eagle; while in Malkhut are the four faces
of a man.

667) "The fourth part of a hin" (Numbers 28:14). This refers to
the fourth leg of the divine Throne, which is Binah, that has
four legs, namely: Hesed, Gevurah and Tipheret of Ze'ir Anpin
and Malkhut. And Malkhut "is a continual burnt-offering"
(ibid. v.6) to Him every single day, and it ascends to the
Divine Thought that has no end; and therefore a burnt-offering
is due only (as an expiation) for sinful meditation of the heart.
(Midrash Vayiqra Rabba 7, 3 — in the name of Rabbi Shimeon
b. Yohai.)

THE FAITHFUL SHEPHERD

668) And in the first part, the Faithful Shepherd said: "This crown that is called zarqa [one of the Biblical cantillation ascents — tr.] is yod, which is the fourth Sephirah to Hesed, Gevurah and Tipheret, i.e. Malkhut. And is called zarqa [root: zayin resh qoph] because it is cast [Hebrew root: zayin resh qoph] as far as the Divine Thought that has no end, as above in the preceding paragraph. So also the being whose name is man, which is Malkhut, and its four faces, which are the four letters of the Tetragrammaton [yod hey waw and hey], are hyphen, shophar, goes, segolta and this is three beasts which are twelve tribes.

COMMENTARY:

Malkhut, for itself, is not fitted to receive upper light, but only after it ascends and is included in Binah does it become a fitting receptacle for the upper intelligences (as above, Bereshit Aleph, page 7). And on the text: "So also the being whose name is man, which is Malkhut...:" hyphen [maqaph], shophar, goes, segolta, which points to the secret that after Malkhut embraces [maqephet] Binah that is called shophar, Malkhut then goes to receive the segol, that is the secret of the three beasts which are twelve tribes. For the three beings are the secret of the three columns, in each one of which are Hesed and Gevurah, Tipheret and Malkhut, coming to a total of twelve. And had it not been for maqeph shophar, i.e. had Malkhut not risen to the level of Binah that is called shophar, it would not have gone to segol, i.e. it would not have been able to receive those intelligences called segolta.

669) The continual burnt-offering is the fourth leg of the Divine Throne, i.e. Malkhut. It is an offering continually on each one of the six Days of Creation, namely: Hesed, Gevurah, Tipheret, Netsach, Hod, and Yesod of Ze'ir Anpin, while on the Sabbath it is a double portion offering (see Numbers ch. 28), so that light and perfection should be added to it, as is fitting — and this we have already learned.

COMMENTARY:

On weekdays, Malkhut ascends with Ze'ir Anpin to Israel Grandfather and Understanding, i.e. one stage, and there is therefore a continual burnt offering on weekdays. But on the Sabbath, Malkhut ascends with Ze'ir Anpin to upper Father and Mother, which is two levels, that is twice that of weekdays, and therefore the additional sacrifice is added to the continual burnt offering.

THE FAITHFUL SHEPHERD

670) In the first part, the Faithful Shepherd said: In six Sephirot Malkhut ascends continually to the waw, which is Ze'ir Anpin, that is taken hold of by them. Ben (the son of) Yah, which is Ze'ir Anpin, having the intelligences of Yah, which is hidden in Binah, and in a certain Sephirah of the six Sephirot that are in Malkhut, i.e. Tipheret of Malkhut that includes all six of its Sephirot, ascends to Ze'ir Anpin. And this is on the third day, i.e. with His third Sephirah, that is called Tipheret, which is also composed of all six of his Sephirot. But

the upper three Sephirot are missing, because although at the time of the offering of the sacrifice, he has the six intermediate Sephirot of Binah, namely Israel Grandfather and Understanding, they are nevertheless not considered as the real intelligences of the upper three Sephirot, for Israel Grandfather and Understanding are also the six intermediate Sephirot of Binah. But on the Sabbath day, added to him is an extra soul [nephesh] which is Binah, i.e. the upper hey of the Tetragrammaton [yod hey waw and hey]; that is: it ascends to upper Father and Mother, namely, the upper three Sephirot of Binah, and then it also has yod, which is the letter, the sign of the Sabbath, i.e. upper Hokhmah; and also the King, which is Ze'ir Anpin, is adorned with a crown [Keter], i.e. Keter, Hokhmah, and Binah of Binah. And for this reason 'A crown they shall give You' is recited in the Additional Service [on the Sabbath day, in the reader's repetition of the shemoneh esreh, during the Kedushah, the third of the 18 blessings, in the Sephardi version only — tr.]

671) "And in your new moons" (Numbers 28:11). [The literal rendering of the verse would be: 'And in the heads (first days) of your moons'— tr.] The question is to be asked: How many heads does the moon have? To which the answer is: There are two points, thus: segol ˙.˙, where the lower dot is the moon, i.e. Malkhut. Its two heads are the two dots over and above it, and together (the three of them) are called segol [the name of 'e' vowel that is written with three dots, placed as at the corners of an equilateral triangle — tr.]. Initially, a crown was over two kings, namely, Netsach and Hod of Ze'ir Anpin, thus: ˙.˙ , which is the form of the segolta as a Biblical cantillation sign [and not a vowel — tr.]; and afterwards, when it said that it is not possible for two kings to use one crown, the Holy One, blessed be He, said to it (the crown): Go and contract yourself, and it descended to the feet of those two kings, i.e. below

Netsach and Hod, thus `·.·` which is a segol [as the vowel 'e' — tr.]. And where it had been a segolta cantillation sign, it became a segol vowel.

COMMENTARY:

Initially, Malkhut was above the chest of Ze'ir Anpin and was attired with the left column of Binah; and Hesed, Gevurah and Tipheret of Ze'ir Anpin enclothed the right column of Binah. It was then in the secret of "the two great lights" (Genesis 1:16), and was as big as Ze'ir Anpin. And since it was above the chest of Ze'ir Anpin, it was understood to have been above Netsach and Hod as in the segolta of the cantillation signs, where the one point, Malkhut, is above the other two points, Netsach and Hod of Ze'ir Anpin, that are now at the corners of the base, and Malkhut is their apex, crown [Keter]. However, it [Malkhut] was unable to stay in this position because of a lack of hasadim, and therefore complained, saying: It is impossible for two kings, i.e. Ze'ir Anpin and Malkhut, to use one crown. It was then said to it [to Malkhut]: Go and contract yourself, and it descended from the chest and downwards of Ze'ir Anpin, below Netsach and Hod. And this is the secret of the segol, that the two points which are Netsach and Hod are on top, while Malkhut is the point that is below them, all of which is thoroughly explained above (see Bereshit Aleph, 110-116). And on the text: "Initially, a crown was over the two kings"; i.e. before the contraction, it [Malkhut] was above the chest of Ze'ir Anpin, and it follows that it was a crown over Netsach and Hod of Ze'ir Anpin. Afterwards, "when it said that it is not possible... it descended to the feet of those two kings" — i.e. it descended to beneath the chest, under Netsach and Hod.

And where it had been a segolta cantillation sign, it became a segol vowel, in the latter of which the two points Netsach and Hod are on the top, and Malkhut is beneath them, below.

672) And the secret of the matter is that corresponding to the two points, which are the two kings, i.e. Netsach and Hod of Ze'ir Anpin, is the Scriptural allusion "two young bullocks (Numbers 28:11);" and corresponding to the one point which is the crown on the head of the two points, the Scripture said "and one ram" (ibid.), there being just one, like a crown. And this is the shape of the segolta cantillation sign, where Malkhut is a crown over Netsach and Hod; and after she said: It is impossible for two kings to use one crown and contracted herself, it [Keter] also contracted "and one he-goat for a sin offering" (cf. ibid. v. 15), for the ram of Isaac, which is the left column of Binah, in which Malkhut enclothed in the first state, contracted and became a he-goat, for it changed from Mercy to Judgement and contracted. For the area above the chest of Ze'ir Anpin is Mercy, and that below the chest of Ze'ir Anpin is Judgement. He therefore contracted from being a ram to being a he-goat, which teaches about Judgement.

673) And this is why the Scripture says: "And one he-goat for a sin offering" (ibid.) and not for a burnt-offering, which would have meant that it ascends to be a crown over Netsach and Hod. And how do we know that there is descent in a sin offering? From the verse: "And he came down from making the sin-offering" (Leviticus 9:22). And why did he combine the sin-offering with the burnt offering in the descent, as it says: "And he came down from making the sin offering and the burnt offering" (ibid.)? This is to teach that initially there was a burnt-offering, which is the attribute of Mercy, i.e. from the

chest and upwards of Ze'ir Anpin, which is the place of Mercy, and later it became Judgement in the descent to below the chest of Ze'ir Anpin, which is the place of Judgement, and is called a sin-offering. And it is all one, for both the burnt-offering and the sin offering are the secret of Malkhut.

674) And this is why the Holy One, blessed be He, who is Ze'ir Anpin, said: Bring atonement over Me, for the moon was certainly a crown over Me, prior to the contraction, i.e. Keter above Netsach and Hod of Ze'ir Anpin, thus: .˙. [as a segolta cantillation sign — tr.], and subsequently it contracted and descended to His feet, i.e. beneath Netsach and Hod, that are called feet, thus: ˙.˙ [as a segol vowel— tr.]. And at the time of bringing over Me atonement, i.e. when the he-goat of the new moon is sacrificed to atone for the contraction of the moon, it is said about it that it is a burnt-offering [olah]; that is that it ascends [olah] from His feet, and it is then said about it: "The earth is My footstool" (Isaiah 66:1), where the earth is Malkhut, and now it rises to be a throne for Binah, together with Ze'ir Anpin, who is called heaven, so that it can be said about it: "The heaven is My throne" (ibid.), for the heavens, which is Ze'ir Anpin together with Malkhut, become a throne for Binah. And this is the secret of the verse "The righteous one rules in the fear of God" (II Samuel 23:3): Judgement becomes Mercy, for by means of the he-goat of the new moon, Hokhmah and hasadim are drawn down to her [to Malkhut], so that she can return to the chest and upwards of Ze'ir Anpin, which is the place of Mercy. This, however, is effective only at the time of the sacrifice, and not subsequently, for this correction is not completed until the end of the correction. And the secret of the matter is contained in the verse: "The stone which the builders rejected is become the chief corner-stone" (Psalms 118:22). And likewise there is the combination: hey waw hey yod, which teaches about the attribute of Judgement, and there is the

combination: yod hey waw hey, that teaches about the attribute of Mercy. And the difference between them is as great as is that between from the chest and upwards and from the chest and downwards, and see above. (Vayigash, page 11.)

675) The one lamb and "two lambs of the first year without blemish" (Numbers 28:9) correspond to the upper three Sephirot. "Seven lambs of the first year" (ibid. v.19) correspond to the seven lower Sephirot. The seven lambs are seven days, i.e. seven Sephirot, of the moon, which is Malkhut, for they are "of the first year [literally: sons of a year]", i.e. the sons of the moon which is called a year, this being one of those primordial years.

COMMENTARY:

This is one of the ten inclusive Sephirot, where Atiq and Sephirot Father and Mother are the secret of Keter; and Father and Mother and Israel Grandfather and understanding are the secret of Hokhmah and Binah; and Ze'ir Anpin is the secret of Tipheret, which includes the six Sephirot Hesed Gevurah, Tipheret, Netsach, Hod and Yesod; and the last one is the secret of Malkhut. Thus Malkhut is one of the ten inclusive Sephirot that are the secret of the primordial years.

676) "And in your new moons [literally: on the heads of your months]" (Numbers 28:11). The question is asked: How many heads is the moon considered to have, since not the moon, but the sun, which is Ze'ir Anpin, is a head, i.e. is a head for it

(the moon)? The answer to this is: There are two heads in every month, namely, Jacob and Joseph, which are Ze'ir Anpin and Yesod, and they are renewed to illuminate the moon, which is Malkhut. And it has, therefore, to be renewed, i.e. with the sacrifices.

677) "Two young bullocks" (Numbers 28:11): These are they about whom the moon said: How can two kings use one crown, i.e. Ze'ir Anpin and Malkhut from the aspect of the two great lights, (Genesis 1:16); and afterwards it contracted itself beneath them, i.e. descended to below the chest of Ze'ir Anpin. "And one ram" (Numbers 28:11) refers to the ram of Isaac (cf. Genesis 22), which is Gevurah. But the question has to be asked: Where did Abraham go? I.e. why is the quality of Abraham, which is Hesed (loving kindness), not mentioned here? It is because Esau awoke there. And who is that? That is the he-goat [se'ir] of the new moon, a part of which is for the evil forces and is called se'ir, just as Esau was "a hairy man" [ish sa'ir] (Genesis 27:11). Therefore Abraham was gathered up, that is to say that there should be no suckling for the evil forces from the light of Hesed, but Isaac, who is the left column, was there because his love for him was as wine with its sediment. For Esau is the refuse of the left column, and the light of the left is called wine, and the refuse is called sediment. Jacob, which is Ze'ir Anpin, the central column, was there in order to cancel the face of Esau, for the central column reduces the upper three Sephirot of the left, which is the face of Esau (as above, Lekh, page 13). Joseph, i.e. Yesod, which is the ox of Ze'ir Anpin, that is to say which is drawn from the left column of Ze'ir Anpin that is called ox, was there for Rachel, i.e. to emanate to Malkhut, that is called Rachel.

THE FAITHFUL SHEPHERD

678) The Faithful Shepherd said: Certainly the one-year-old lambs are named after the sun, which is Holy Mother, i.e. Binah, for it is said about it: The face of Moses is as that of the sun. (Cf. Talmud Bavli, Baba Batra, 75a.), that is, he had the upper three Sephirot, which is the secret of face, of Binah, that is called sun. A year contains 365 days [on the Hebrew lunar calendar, the twelve months have a maximum of 355 days, to which are added the ten days from the New Year until the Day of Atonement, i.e. these ten days are both part of the new year and are added on to the previous year, thus making 365 days in a year — tr.]. This is the same number, 365, as that of the negative precepts. And this is 'ed (witness) for the left, and is upper Mother. The moon, which is Malkhut, is on the right side, for the daughter is joined to Father, which is Hesed, on the right side. And it, Malkhut, is composed of the 248 positive precepts. It follows that the waw, which is Ze'ir Anpin, is with Mother on the left side, in the secret of the 365 negative precepts, and the daughter is with Father on the right side, which is Hesed. And the secret of the matter is in the verse: "By wisdom [Hokhmah] He founded the earth" (Proverbs 3:19). By wisdom refers to Father, i.e. Hokhmah of the right which is Hesed (as above, 204). Earth is the daughter, i.e. Malkhut, and thus the daughter is joined with Father. "By understanding He established the heavens" (ibid.). Established the heavens is the son, i.e. Ze'ir Anpin, with Mother, which is Understanding. And this results in the combination of the Tetragrammaton [yod, hey, hey, waw], which is the secret of the heavenly essences in the center.

COMMENTARY:

The author here gives an exposition of the seven lambs that
differs from that which he gave above (675), when he said that
they are seven Sephirot of the moon. Here he says that they
correspond to seven Sephirot of the sun, which is Ze'ir Anpin.
And on the text: The "one-year-old lambs are named after the
sun, which is Holy Mother," i.e. after Ze'ir Anpin, that is
called the light of the sun which receives from Holy Mother,
for, from the point of view of the light of the left that Ze'ir
Anpin receives from Holy Mother, it is called sun. And on the
text: "For it is said about it: The face of Moses," which is Ze'ir
Anpin, "is as that of the sun:" For then, when it receives from
Mother, its face is discerned as the light of the sun in its
might. A year — i.e. a solar year, contains 365 days, which is
the same number as that of the negative precepts. For 365
negative precepts is the secret of the intelligences of the left.
And on the text: "And this is 'ed (witness) for the left:" The
intelligences are termed Eden and 'ed. And he says that the
intelligences of the 365 days of the solar year are witness for
the left, i.e. the illumination of Hokhmah that is on the left
side, "Upper Mother" for they are drawn down from upper
Mother. And these seven one-year-old lambs that he sacrifices
are parallel to seven Sephirot of Ze'ir Anpin, for they draw to
it the illumination of Hokhmah that is on the left side of
Mother, this being the secret of one-year-olds, from the 365
days of the solar year, which are the intelligences of the left
side of Mother. But "the moon, which is Malkhut, is on the
right side, for the daughter is joined to the Father, which is
Hesed:" For Malkhut is connected to the intelligences of Father,
which is Hokhmah of the right side, which is the light of
hasadim, for Hokhmah itself within her is hidden and
concealed, illuminating only in the light of Hesed, as above
(204, q.v.). "And it, Malkhut, is composed of the 248 positive

precepts," which are Hesed. And it follows that by the
sacrificial offering of the new moon each one receives what it
is lacking. For Ze'ir Anpin originates in hasadim without
Hokhmah, and it now therefore receives, by the sacrifice,
Hokhmah of the left side, which is from Mother. And
Malkhut, which originates in Hokhmah of the left side, and
lacks only hasadim, receives hasadim from upper Father. And
on the text: "It follows that the waw, which is Ze'ir Anpin, is
with Mother on the left side," for it receives Hokhmah of the
left side from Mother, which was what it lacked. "The daughter
is with the Father on the right side, which is Hesed:" And the
daughter is to be found with Father, which is Hokhmah of the
right side, which is Hesed, which is what she lacked. And on
the text: "And this results in the combination of the
Tetragrammaton" [yod hey waw and hey] but with the letters in
the order: yod hey hey waw, for the lower hey which is
Malkhut comes after the yod, which is Father, and the upper
hey, which is Mother, is before the waw, which is Ze'ir Anpin.
"The heavenly essences in the center:" This is said in the secret
of the four sections of the phylacteries, which is the secret of
the Tetragrammaton [yod hey waw and hey] with the letters in
the correct order: yod is kadesh; upper hey is "And it shall be,
when the Lord your God shall bring you in" (Deuteronomy
6:10); waw is the Shema Israel ("Hear, O Israel, the Lord our
God, the Lord is One" — Deuteronomy 6:4); and lower hey is
"And it will come to pass if you will diligently hearken"
(Deuteronomy 11:13 — the middle paragraph of the Shema
Israel), as is explained above. (In the Introduction to Sepher
ha-Zohar, from 238 — 242). However, from the aspect of the
above order of Father established the daughter, the two
paragraphs starting with the letters of the Tetragrammaton,
[And it shall come to pass = ve'hayah: waw hey yod hey],
namely "And it shall come to pass when the Lord your God
bring you in" and "And it shall come to pass if you will

diligently hearken," are in the middle, for they are the secret of the two heys, while kadesh, which is the secret of the yod is earlier, and Shema Israel, which is the secret of waw is at the end, i.e. in the order: yod hey hey waw.

679) Again: "One he-goat for a sin-offering" (Numbers 29:11). There are two goats, as it is said about them: "And he shall take the two goats... one lot for the Lord and the other lot for Azazel" (Leviticus 16:7-8). The goat that is for the Lord is an atonement over the contraction of the moon (as above, 674) and is "One he-goat for a sin-offering to the Lord" (Numbers 28:15). It is therefore referred to as 'one' [echad] because it is from the side of the unity [yichud]. But the goat for Azazel is not referred to as 'one,' neither is it called a sacrifice, a fire offering, nor a burnt-offering, but shall be sent "away by the hand of an appointed man into the wilderness" (Leviticus 16:21). "And shall send away" is the same term used by Jacob: "It is a present sent to my lord, even to Esau" (Genesis 32:19). Likewise, the goat for Azazel is a bribe, in order to break Samael's anger that he should not draw near the Temple, to offer a case against it. (As above, Noach, 104.)

680) It is as with a hungry dog... whoever does not want to be bitten by it gives it meat or bread to eat and water to drink. And the secret of the matter is contained in the verse: "If your enemy be hungry give him bread to eat, and if he be thirsty, give him water to drink" (Proverbs 25:21). He thereby becomes friendly towards the person, and not only does not bite him, with a number of tribulations, but becomes an advocate for him and loves him. (As above, Noach, 104.)

681) And there is a question here: Why is the goat sent to

Azazel by the hand of an appointed man who is disabled? The answer is because all of the evil forces are disabled, and are called goats, as it is written: "And goats shall dance there" (Isaiah 13:21). And about them it is said: "And they shall no more sacrifice their sacrifices to the goats" (Leviticus 17:7); and also: "They sacrificed to demons, no-gods" (Deuteronomy 32:17). And with this goat to Azazel, Samael is separated from everything and bears all the transgressions that are in Israel upon him, as it is written: "And the goat shall bear upon him all their iniquities" (Leviticus 16:22). And futhermore, after Azazel takes all the transgressions, Scripture says "And shall bear," i.e. that the Holy One, blessed be He, shall bear and forgive. The Holy One, blessed be He, is called "bearing (= forgiving) iniquity" (Exodus 34:7), and about the goat for Azazel it is written: "And the goat shall bear upon him all their iniquities" (Leviticus 16:22). What is the difference between these two types of bearing? The answer to this question is that in the case of the goat, bearing means bearing a burden, carrying, while in the case of the Holy One, blessed be He, bearing means the removal of the burden, i.e. that He atones the iniquities. And all of this is explained above (Acharey Mot, page 40).

682) That is its three first stages, namely Keter, Hokhmah, and Binah, each one of which is made up of ten, as it is above, with Ze'ir Anpin; and by tenths is meant one part in ten, for Malkhut is one of the ten Sephirot of Ze'ir Anpin, and each of its Sephirot is in detail one of ten that correspond to it in Ze'ir Anpin, and they are therefore called tenths. And one goat for a sin-offering. Why is it called a sin-offering? Because it is a sin and is from the side of sin, that is to say: a portion of it is for the evil forces, and it is therefore from the side of sin. Said Rabbi Elazar: But it is written: "To the Lord (Numbers 28:15)!" How then can you say that it is from the side of sin?! The answer to this is that it is certainly sacrificed to the Lord,

for it is written: To make atonement, i.e. to break the face of the evil forces, and everything will be sacrificed to the Sanctuary, but one portion is also given to Samael, and he eats it, and for this reason does not take hold of the other sacrifices. This sacrifice alone is for him to eat, and no other sacrifice is joined with it for him to eat.

683) He, Samael, enjoys the banquet of the King with this portion that he takes from the goat for Azazel, and he therefore rejoices and leaves Israel alone and does not accuse them. And were it not for contraction of the moon, i.e. Malkhut (as explained above, Bereshit Aleph 110 — 115), nothing at all would be given to Samael from the King's banquet. And what does he do in the contraction of the moon? Because he comes close and suckles from the vacated place in Malkhut, and takes power for his people from the side of the left of the moon, which is Malkhut, and grows strong in it, and in this goat, a portion of which is given to him, he abandons everything and gains his enjoyment from this. And because the Holy One, blessed be He, contracted the moon, for He said to her 'Go and contract yourself' (as explained there), therefore this goat is sacrificed, so that Samael will depart from her and not come close to the Sanctuary, which is Malkhut. And thus we learned that the Holy One, blessed be He, said: Bring over Me an atonement, for I have contracted the moon. 'Over me', i.e. because of Me, for I contracted her, and it is my fault that I contracted her, that you need this, that you need to sacrifice a goat in order to separate him (Samael) from the place of the contraction of Malkhut. (And these matters are explained above, Noach, 103 — 104.)

THE FAITHFUL SHEPHERD

684) "And in your new moons [literally: And in the heads of

your moons]" (Numbers 28:11). The word 'heads' is written in the plural, referring to Jacob and Joseph, i.e. Ze'ir Anpin and Yesod, as it is written: "These are the generations of Jacob. Joseph..." (Genesis 37:2) that renew the moon, which is Malkhut. I have found in the Book of Enoch that he said that just as on the first day of the month the moon, which is Malkhut, is purified to come close to her husband, Ze'ir Anpin (as explained in Noach, 103-104), so must one portion be given to the evil forces (as is explained there) — and from the same type as the evil forces, i.e. a goat; so also the woman when she is purified for her husband, one portion must be given to the evil forces, and from their type.

685) And what is that portion that the woman has to give to the evil forces? It is the finger-nails with their dirt and a little of the ends of her hair, for she has to comb her head and tie her hair together, to give them to the evil forces, and then that evil side will not go after her to harm her, but will leave her alone from all sides. And what does she do with those hairs and nail clippings? After she has bound them together, she has to place them where people do not pass by, or in holes in the bottom of the yard, and conceal them there.

686) Again: "And in your new moons" (Numbers 28:11). The sages of the Mishnah said: When the new moon used to be sanctified by the court, flares used to be kindled on the tops of the mountains (Mishnah, Rosh ha-Shanah 2, 2-3.), and they used to say: Thus has he seen it, and sanctified it. (Cf. Talmud Bavli, Rosh ha-Shanah 20a.) The moon would be banana-shaped, sometime with the ends looking upwards, and sometime looking downwards, sometime to the east and sometime to the west, sometime to the south and sometime to the north. And this is its looking in six directions that Tipheret, which is a large waw, encompasses, namely: Gedulah,

Gevurah, Tipheret, Netsach, Hod, and Yesod. Gedulah, which is Hesed, is its looking to the south, and its looking to the north is Gevurah, to the east is Tipheret, and to the west is Yesod.

687) The point that is drawn out of the moon, which is Malkhut, from the inside, is Hokhmah, and the line that circumvents the moon is Keter. And as a rule that point, which is Malkhut, is sometimes a diadem for Ze'ir Anpin, in the secret of the verse: "A virtuous woman is a diadem to her husband" (Proverbs 12:4), and sometimes a throne for Ze'ir Anpin to sit upon, and at yet other times a stool (that serves) for a footstool for Ze'ir Anpin.

688) Why is Malkhut called moon? The answer to this is the word moon [l'vanah, root: lamed beit nun] comes from clarification [libun, root: lamed beit nun] of the Halakhah, i.e. it is named after Hokhmah of the right side that clarifies the Halakhah, for it is Malkhut that is called Halakhah, for Hokhmah is from within Malkhut, in the secret of the verse: "All glorious is the king's daughter within (the palace)" (Psalms 45:14) and it is purified [root: lamed beit nun] in the fire of Binah that descends upon it. And the secret of the matter is to be found in the verse: "Though your sins be as scarlet, they shall be as white [root: lamed beit nun] as snow" (Isaiah 1:18). And whereas it was 'The Lord' [aleph dalet nun yod], the letters of which, re-arranged, spell dina [dalet yod nun aleph], Judgement [in Aramaic — tr.], which is red with Gevurah (might), i.e. with the left column where Binah is, it becomes purified, whitened [root: lamed beit nun] from the side of Hesed where Hokhmah is, and returns to the Name of the Tetragrammaton [yod hey waw and hey], which is Mercy.

COMMENTARY:

From Binah it receives Hokhmah of the left side, and from Hokhmah of the right side it receives hasadim, and is purified, whitened in the strength of both of them, in the secret of the verse: "Though your sins be as scarlet, they shall be as white as snow" (Isaiah 1:18).

689) And what is the cause of Malkhut's changing from Judgement to Mercy? This is the completely righteous, for the moon, which is Malkhut is from the side of the Tree of Knowledge of Good and Evil (see Genesis 2:17). Its shell is darkness in the secret of "if it is a bright black spot," which is the evil inclination, which is a bondwoman, about whom it is said: "And it be not lower (than the skin), but be dim" (Leviticus 13:21). And Malkhut has nothing of its own, but only that line that gives it light, this being the secret of a line of Hokhmah of the left side without hasadim, which is primarily in Binah, but its light is as thin as a line because it cannot illuminate without hasadim. For it accompanies it during the night-time, which is the Exile, in the secret of the verse: "She rises also while it is yet night" (Proverbs 31:15) and leaves it during the day. For the day is the time of the rule of the hasadim of Ze'ir Anpin, and Hokhmah of the left side is unable to rule by day, for daytime is the light of Hesed of the next world, which is Binah, in which "But to you who fear My name shall the sun of righteousness arise with healing in its wings" (Malakhi 3:20).

690) But that point that is within the moon, which is Malkhut, that is from the side of the Tree of Life, which is Ze'ir Anpin, is the secret of Hokhmah of the right side, which is Hesed, and

is as a never ceasing spring, because it is drawn down from upper Father and Mother by way of Ze'ir Anpin, whose coupling never ceases, and about which it is written: "And like a spring of water, whose waters fail not" (Isaiah 58:11), and it is called "a lovely kind" (Proverbs 5:19) from the side of Hesed (loving kindness), which is love, this being as is written: "With an everlasting love have I loved you; therefore with Hesed (affection) have I drawn you" (Jeremiah 31:3), love being the secret of Hesed; and it has two beams from the light, thus: U — and sometimes "the one is higher than the other" J (Daniel 8:13), and at other times they are equal.

COMMENTARY:

The beams are the illumination of Netsach and Hod of Ze'ir Anpin, and thus the right hand beam, which is Netsach, is higher than the left hand beam, which is Hod. And this is the secret of the verse: "But one was higher than the other" (Daniel 8:3). And it is known that Ze'ir Anpin and Malkhut are the secret of Netsach and Hod, since they enclothe Netsach and Hod of Arikh Anpin. Therefore, when Ze'ir Anpin and Malkhut are face to face, at the same height, Netsach and Hod of Ze'ir Anpin, are also at the same height, and Netsach is not higher than Hod. And then the beams of Malkhut are also at the same height, as the text says: At other times they are equal, i.e. when Male and Female are at the same height.

THE MORNING STAR

691) "And in the first month" (Numbers 28:16). Rabbi Abba opened the discussion by quoting the verse: "As the hart pants after the water brooks, so pants my soul after You, O God" (Psalms 42:2). We have already learned this verse, and although it contains both masculine and feminine forms, it is all one, for the word ayyil (hart) is masculine, while the verb ta'arog (pants) is feminine, and although according to the rules of grammar, the subject and the verb should agree in gender, ya'arog (pants) is not written in the masculine — because it is all one. In other words, Malkhut, when in the first state, when it is with Ze'ir Anpin, in the secret of the two large lights, is called hart [ayyil], this being a masculine form, but in the second state, after it has contracted, it is called hind [ayyalah], this being a feminine form.

692) What is ayyelet ha-shachar (the morning star, but literally: the hind of the dawn) (Psalms 22:1)? This is a certain merciful one, i.e. Malkhut, and amongst all the beings of the world there is none merciful like her, for when time is pressing and she needs nourishment for herself and for all the beings, which are all the hosts of the worlds of Beriah, Yetsirah, and Asiyah, she goes to a distant place, far away, and comes, bringing food, but does not herself want to eat until she returns to her place. Why is this so? So that all the other beings will collect together by her, and she distributes that food to them. And when she comes, all the other beings do indeed collect around her, and she stands in the middle, and allocates to each one of them. And the sign is in the verse: "She rises also while it is yet night, and gives food to her household, and a portion to her maidens" (Proverbs 31:15). And from what she gives to them she is herself satiated, as if she had eaten more food than all of them.

693) And when the morning, which is called shachar (dawn) arrives, the pangs of the Exile come to her, and this is why she is called ayyelet ha-shachar (literally: hind of the dawn), after the blackness of the morning, for she then has pangs as a woman with child, as it is written: "Like as a woman with child, whose time of delivery draws near, is in pain and cries out in her pangs" (Isaiah 26:17).

694) When does she distribute (the food) to them? This is when the morning is just about to come, but it is still night, and the blackness departs for the illumination, as it is written: "She rises also while it is yet night, and gives food to her household" (Proverbs 31:15). But by the time it is morning, they are all satiated with her food.

695) And then a certain voice awakens in the midst of the firmament and calls out aloud, saying: Let those who are near, go to their places; let those who are far, leave. Let each one go to his rightful place. And by the time the sun shines, each one is gathered to his place, as it is written: "The sun rises, they are gathered up" (Psalms 104:22). And she departs during the day, and is revealed at night, and distributes food in the morning, which is why she is called ayyelet ha-shachar (morning star, literally: the hind of the dawn).

696) Subsequently, she grows stronger and goes and is called ayyil (hart), i.e. a masculine form. To what place does she go? The answer to this is that she goes sixty parasangs [one parasang is about 4 miles — tr.] from that place that she left and she enters into the mountain of darkness. And she goes into the mountain of darkness, a certain labyrinthine serpent sniffs at her feet and follows her, and she ascends from there to the mountain of light. When she reaches there, the Holy One, blessed be He, arranges for her another serpent, who

goes forth and they fight each other, and she is saved. And from there she takes food, and returns to her place by midnight. And from midnight on, she begins the distribution, until the blackness of the morning arises. And when the morning gives light, she goes from there and is no longer visible, as we have learned.

697) And when the world is in need of rain, all the other beings collect by her, and she goes up to the top of a high mountain, wraps her head between her knees, and cries out with one long shout after another. And the Holy One, blessed be He, hears her voice, and is overcome by mercy and has pity on the world. And she comes down from the top of the mountain, and runs to hide herself. And all the other beings run after her, but do not find her. This is as it is written: "As the hart pants after the water brooks" (Psalms 42:2). What is the meaning of "after the water brooks"? This refers to those water brooks that have dried up, and the world is thirsty for water. Then "it pants."

698)   When she conceives, she is closed up, but when the time comes for her to give birth, she shouts and cries out, cry after cry, up to 70 shouts, as the number of words in the psalm: "The Lord answer you in the day of trouble" (Psalms 20:2) [there are exactly seventy words in the Hebrew psalm — tr.], which is the song of this pregnant one. And the Holy One, blessed be He, hears her, and arranges for her salvation. And then a certain large serpent emerges from the mountains of darkness, and comes between the mountains, its mouth licking the dust (cf. Michah 7:17) and it reaches this hart [ayyil] and comes and bites it twice in the same place.

699) On the first occasion, blood comes out of it, and the serpent licks (it). On the second occasion, water comes out,

and all those animals of the mountains drink (of it), and she herself is opened and gives birth. And a sign for you is the verse: "And (he) smote the rock with his rod twice, and water came froth abundantly, and the congregation drank and their cattle" (Numbers 20:11).

700) At that time The Holy One, blessed be He, has pity on her because of what the serpent did, as it is written: "The voice of the Lord makes the hinds to calve, and strips the forests bare; and in His temple, all say: Glory." (Psalms 29:9). "The voice of the Lord makes the hinds to calve" refers to the pangs and pains that give rise to those 70 shouts, as above. And then follows "and strips the forests bare" in order to awaken that serpent, and reveal the being that is going amongst them. "And in His temple." What does this mean? It refers to the temple of the Holy One, blessed be He, which is Malkhut, in which all those multitudes that are in the worlds of Beriah, Yetsirah, and Asiyah open and say: Glory! What is meant by glory? It refers to "Blessed be the glory of the Lord from His place" (Ezekiel 3:12), which is Malkhut that is called the glory of the Lord.

COMMENTARY:

The Zohar here explains to us a certain profound matter regrading Malkhut, and the explanation has four aspects.

a) (692-697) How she distributes food in terms of the illumination of Hokhmah to all her hosts, in the secret of the verse: "She rises also while it is yet night, and gives food to her household (Proverbs 31:15)."

b) (692-697) The secret of the midnight mating, and the order of the corrections that she receives.

c) (697-698) The matter of the opening of the emanation of water that is in Malkhut, namely, Hasadim.

d) (698-701) The matter of the birth of souls [neshamah], and the smiting of the rock.

And you already know that Ze'ir Anpin is the secret of the rule by day, and is the secret of the right side, which is the rule of hasadim. And Malkhut is the secret of the rule by night, and is the secret of the left side, which is the rule of Hokhmah that is on the left side. And this has been stated in a number of places. Consequently, Malkhut during the daytime, when Hokhmah is unable to control, is pressed for time and has no food of her own, which is the secret of the light of Hokhmah of the left side. And on the text (692): "When time is pressing," i.e. during the daylight hours, for there is then no revelation for the light of Hokhmah which is food for her and all her hosts that are drawn down from her. "And she needs nourishment for herself and for all the beings:" For she needs to draw down her food. "She goes to a distant place, far away:" For Hokhmah is emanated only with judgments, and so long as she is not enclothed with hasadim in the secret of the mating of the central column, harsh judgments are drawn from her, as has been stated in a number of places, and these judgments, which are revealed upon her appearance, are compared to a distant place and to far away. This is the secret of the verse: "And his sister stood afar off" (Exodus 2:4), where his sister alludes to Hokhmah. Likewise: "I said: I will get wisdom, but it was far from me" (Ecclesiastes 7:23). And this she does immediately at the beginning of the night, and the darkness

therefore spreads them over the earth, for the illumination of
Hokhmah of the left side without the right side is darkness (as
above, Bereshit Aleph, page 47), but then her food, which is
the illumination of Hokhmah, is drawn down. And on the text:
"And comes, bringing food:" For she then brings the food,
which is the secret of Hokhmah of the left side. But at that
juncture, while she is drawing down the Hokhmah, she freezes
because of the many judgments that are in Hokhmah without
hasadim, which means that she is unable to emanate a thing, as
was explained above (Bereshit Aleph, page 247). And on the
text: "But does not herself want to eat until she returns to her
place:" For Malkhut does not want to be in the aspect of the
left side without the right side in the place where Hokhmah
emerges, this being the secret of far away, as above, until she
returns to her place, which is the central column of Ze'ir
Anpin, where there is unity of the left side with the right side,
for this is her permanent place, between the two arms of the
King. And the Zohar asks: Why is this so? Why does she have
to return to her place? And gives the answer: "So that all the
other beings will collect together by her, and she distributes
that food to them." For prior to her coming to her place in the
central column, her lights are frozen and she is unable to
emanate a thing to the other beings, i.e. to her hosts who are
drawn down from her. But when she returns to her place all
the beings gather to her, and she emanates the light of
Hokhmah to them. And on the text: "And when she comes, all
the other beings do indeed collect around her, and she stands in
the middle" — i.e. she stands in the mating with the central
column. "And allocates to each one of them:" For then, when
she is in the central column, her lights are opened and she can
distribute to each one of them. And receipt of the light of
Hokhmah is termed 'rising.' And on the text: "And the sign is
in the verse: "She rises also while it is yet night and gives food
to her household and a portion to her maidens'" (Proverbs

31:15). "She rises also while it is yet night," i.e. she then receives Hokhmah which is termed 'rising.' "And gives food to her household," i.e. she emanates to all her hosts. And it is known that when Hokhmah illuminates on the left side without the right side, it gives light in the upper three Sephirot of Hokhmah. But after the central column unites the left side with the right side, the upper three Sephirot of Hokhmah of the left side contract, and Hokhmah of the left side illuminates only in the aspect of upwards from below, this being the secret of the six intermediate Sephirot of Hokhmah, as above (Bereshit Aleph, page 60). And it follows that before Malkhut comes to her place, which is the central column, she illuminates the upper three Sephirot of Hokhmah of the left, but now that she has come to her place, to the central column, she has contracted to the six intermediate Sephirot of Hokhmah. And on the text: "And from what she gives to them she is herself satiated, as if she had eaten more food than all of them." That is to say, although she has now contracted to the central column, in the aspect of the six intermediate Sephirot of Hokhmah, and is unable to eat, i.e. to receive the upper three Sephirot of Hokhmah, she has no pain from this, but, on the contrary, now that she is able to distribute the emanation of Hokhmah to her hosts, she is more satisfied than if she had eaten more than all of them, i.e. than when she ate from the upper three Sephirot of Hokhmah. For this is a most important foodstuff, because previously her lights had been frozen and she had been unable to emanate a thing, as above. This is now no longer the case, for she emanates to all her hosts.

And on the text (693): "And when the morning, which is called shachar (dawn) arrives," i.e. when the dawn has to arrive, which is the secret of midnight (as is explained here, 696). "The pangs of Exile come to her;" i.e. the judgments of the left side without the right side, which are the pangs of the Exile, and, for this reason, she returns to her place to the central column, at midnight, for she does not want to stand in these judgments. "And this is why she is called ayyelet ha-shachar (literally: hind of the dawn) after the blackness of the morning," as above, for she has pangs as a woman in childbirth, for the secret of birth pangs is that they are also from these judgments of the control of the left side (as is clarified below).

And on the text (694): "When does she distribute (the food) to them? This is when the morning is just about to come, but it is still night, and the blackness departs for the illumination;" i.e. from midnight until the morning, this being the time when Hokhmah emanates to her hosts (as is explained below, 696). However, the illumination of Hokhmah is completed only when it is enclothed in hasadim, whose time is during the rule of the day, which is the light of the morning. And on the text: "But by the time it is morning;" i.e. that the light of Hesed, which is called the light of the morning, illuminates. "They are all satiated with her food:" For Hokhmah is then enclothed in hasadim, and is completed.

And on the text (695): "And then a certain voice awakens in the midst of the firmament;" i.e. a voice from the central column, which is Ze'ir Anpin, whose control now commences, being the rule of the day, i.e. hasadim. "And calls out aloud, saying: Let those who are near go to their places." Those who are drawn down from the right side, which is Hesed, are called 'those who are near,' and it (the voice) therefore says to them that they should enter their places in order to receive Hesed, as the emanation of Hesed commences at this juncture. "Let those who are far, leave:" Those who are drawn down from the left column, where the emanation of Hokhmah is, are called 'those who are far,' after Hokhmah, which is distant (as above, in the commentary to 692), and to them it (the voice) says: Leave, for there is now no emanation of Hokhmah, as needed by those who are far, for it is the rule of the daytime. "Let each one go to his rightful place." Each one will receive according to his root in the three columns. "And by the time the sun shines:" after the sun, which rules by day, has emerged. "Each one is gathered to his place:" each one cleaves to its own root in order to receive its emanation. "And she departs during the day:" For Malkhut leaves during the daytime, which is not the time for her emanation. "And is revealed at night:" For her emanation, which is Hokhmah of the left side, is revealed only by night, as above. "And distributes food in the morning:" That is to say, at the time of preparation of the light of the morning, i.e. from midnight until the dawn. "Which is why she is called ayyelet ha-shachar (morning star, literally: the hind of the dawn):" Because the time of her illumination is at the dawn which begins at midnight, as explained below, but once the sun shines, she departs, and does not emanate a thing all day long from the aspect of Hokhmah of the left side that is assigned to her. And although she emanates hasadim, this is not considered her emanation, but that of Ze'ir Anpin.

And on the text (696): "Subsequently;" i.e. after the rule of day has terminated. "She grows stronger and goes;" i.e. She returns to cleave to the left column that is called Gevurah (might), and goes. "To what place does she go? The answer to this is that she goes sixty parasangs... from that... place that she left;" i.e. she ascends from her place, which is the aspect from the chest and downwards of Ze'ir Anpin, to the place above the chest, where the left column from Mother illuminates, and is able to cleave to the left column and receive Hokhmah. And from the chest and downwards of Ze'ir Anpin are the six Sephirot Hesed, Gevurah, Tipheret, Netsach, Hod, and Yesod, each one of which is composed of ten Sephirot. And she comes to above the chest of Ze'ir Anpin, and cleaves there to the illumination of Hokhmah that is on the left side of Mother, and since she cleaves to the left side only, without the right side, she cleaves to the darkness, for the left side without the right side is darkness (as above, Bereshit Aleph, page 47). And on the text: "And as she goes into the mountain of darkness:" For the left column without the right is the mountain of darkness. "And as she goes into the mountain of darkness, a certain labyrinthine serpent sniffs at her feet and follows:" While she is going in the mountain, the darkness goes after her as a serpent and traces her steps, this being the secret of the judgments of Female that are added to the judgments of the left, until Malkhut is no longer able to bear them, and she returns to her place, to the central column (as above, in the commentary to 693). And on the text: "And she ascends from there to the mountain of light:" She therefore ascends from there to the mountain of light, which is Ze'ir Anpin, which is the central column. And it is known that when the judgments of the left and the judgments of the Female are added to each other, there is none that can withstand them. However, by means of the correction of the central column, they annul each other, inasmuch as they are two opposites. (As is clarified in Acharey Mot, page 39 and Vayera, page 19 and Tazria, 153.)

And on the text: "When she reaches there:" When Malkhut reaches the mountain of light, which is the central column. "The Holy One, blessed be He, arranges for her another serpent," i.e. from the laws of the left side. "Who goes forth and they fight each other:" The judgments of the left fight with the judgments of the Female, since they are opposites of each other, and they thereby annul each other. "And she is saved:"

And Malkhut is saved from all the judgments, both the judgments of the left and the judgments of the Female. And these corrections are undertaken for her at midnight. And on the text: "And from there." From the mountain of light which is where the illumination of Hokhmah is. "She takes food and returns to her place;" to the central column, as above. "By midnight," for this is the time for all the corrections, as above. "And from midnight on, she begins the distribution:" For she then cleaves to the central column, and her lights, which are frozen, as above, are opened, and she is therefore able to emanate and distribute to all her hosts. "Until the blackness of the morning arises;" until the blackness of the morning departs. "And when the morning gives light, she goes from there and is no longer visible:" For with the light of the day commences the rule of Ze'ir Anpin, which is hasadim, and the rule of Malkhut, which is Hokhmah, departs and is not visible all day long.

And on the text (697): "And when the world is in need of rain;" i.e. when the lower beings, through their iniquities, cause a separation between Ze'ir Anpin and Malkhut, and Malkhut no longer cleaves to the central column, then her lights again become frozen, and no rain or dew is drawn downwards from her. "All the other beings collect by her," i.e. they demand an emanation from her. "And she goes up to the top of a high mountain;" i.e. to the above-mentioned mountain of darkness, which is the left column without the right. "And wraps her head between her knees;" i.e. her upper three Sephirot, which are called head, descend to be in the aspect of knees, which are the rear portions and judgments. "And cries out with one long shout after another;" i.e. because of the pangs and the judgments that rest there. "And the Holy One, blessed be He, hears her voice;" i.e. He opens the illumination of hasadim which are called waters. "And she comes down from the top of

the mountain," i.e. she descends from the left column. "And
runs to hide herself; i.e.because the Holy One, blessed be He,
has opened the control of hasadim, which is the secret of the
waters, Malkhut hides, because of the aspect of the
illumination of the left side that she contains, just as she hides
during the daytime. "And all the other run after her, but do
not find her." For since the rule of hasadim has started, giving
water to the world, therefore the illumination of Hokhmah that
is in Malkhut is not to be found. This is as is written: "As the
hart pants after the water brooks" (Psalms 42:2). "Those water
brooks that have dried up; i.e. When she clove to the left side,
her water brooks dried up." And the world is thirsty for water.
Then "it pants." For then she pants after the emanation of the
waters, which are hasadim, as explained.

And on the text (698): "When she conceives, she is closed up."
For when Malkhut is pregnant with the souls (Neshamot) of the
righteous, she receives Male Waters from him, and she sends up
Female Waters, the soul being formed from the two of them,
and then Malkhut arouses the illumination of Hokhmah of the
left side for the sake of the soul (neshamah). And since the
control of the left has been aroused, her lights are again
frozen, as above and she is closed up. Then nothing issues forth
from her to the lower beings. "When she conceives, she is
closed up,"i.e. her lights are frozen within her. "But when the
time comes for her to give birth, she shouts and cries out;"
because she is unable to give birth, everything being congealed
within her. And the secret of the 70 shouts is an allusion to the
judgments that are drawn down from Hokhmah of the left
side, for Hokhmah is called ayyin (meaning an eye, but also the
name of the letter whose numerical value is 70 — tr.). "And
then a certain large serpent emerges from the mountains of
darkness;" i.e. The Holy One, blessed be He, awakens over her
judgments of the Female from the aspect of the Curtain of
Chireq, reducing Gar of the left. This is the secret of "biting."

"And it reaches this hart (Ayyil) and comes and bites it twice," there are two judgments of the Female in the curtain of Chireq, which are the secrets of the Lock and the Key in order to reduce the left column and unite it with the right, where the principal part of the reducing force is the Lock, which is the curtain of Chireq from the aspect of Malkhut of the first contraction, Tsimtsum I. However, so that she may be fitted to receive, in any event, the six intermediate Sephirot of Hokhmah, it is necessary to awaken over her the power of the curtain of Chireq, from the aspect of the Key, which is judgments mitigated by Binah [all of which is clarified at length above, Lekh, page 13,q.v.]. And on the text: "And bites it twice in the same place." Initially from the judgments of the Lock and subsequently from the judgments of the Key. And on the text (699): "On the first occasion;" which is from the aspect of the curtain of the Lock. "Blood comes out of it, and the serpent licks (it);" i.e. he removes the lights from her and licks them; that is to say that this is not just a question of the contraction of the upper three Sephirot, but that she is not fitting to receive and to emanate the lights of the correction, which are the secret of the waters, because the Lock removes all the lights with which it comes into contact (as explained there); and so that she might be corrected and made fitting for the emanation of the waters, she needs the judgments of the Female in the aspect of the Key. And on the text; "On the second occasion;" which is the bite of the judgments from the aspect of Key. "Water comes out and all those animals of the mountains drink." For, by means of the second bite of the Key, she received her correction to emanate the waters, which are the secret of hasadim, and she also received her correction so that she can give birth, for she has been opened up from her closure. This is the meaning of the text 'she opened and gave birth.' And on the text: "And a sign for you is the verse: 'And (he) smote the rock with his rod twice, and water came forth abundantly, and the congregation drank and their cattle.'

(Numbers 20:11)." "And he smote the rock with his rod twice," which is also by means of the above-mentioned two types of judgments, of the Lock and of the Key. And it is written: "And the congregation drank and their cattle." It was necessary to state this twice for the above-mentioned reason, for the Lock acts for the contraction of the upper three Sephirot of the left side, but it is not fitting for placing there light for this reason. And therefore the Key is also required, for from it a receptacle is made for her for the lights of the correction (as is clarified in Lekh, ibid.), which is the secret of waters. It was therefore necessary to smite the rock twice. And you will understand that the rock is Malkhut and that the thirst for water is caused by the iniquities of the lower beings who misdirected Malkhut to cleave to the left. To return to the central column so that she would again give water, it was necessary that Moses, who is the secret of the central column, should smite her twice with the rod, i.e. with the Lock and with the Key. And then: "And the congregation drank and their cattle" (Numbers 20:11).

And on the text (700):" The voice of the Lord makes the hinds to calve" refers to the pangs and pains; these are the secrets of the judgments because of the cleaving to the left side. "And strips the forests bare" in order to awaken that serpent," i.e. to arouse the judgments of the Female from the curtain of Chireq. "And reveal that being that is going amongst them;" for thereby is revealed the emanating power of Malkhut vis-a-vis the lower beings, as above. And then all the hosts say: Blessed be the glory of the Lord from His Place" (Ezekiel 3:12).

THE FAITHFUL SHEPHERD

701) (The beginning of this section is omitted.) One might

suggest that after seventy years she will feel the pains of the birthpangs and in two years she will give birth to the Redemption, one thousand and two hundred years after the Destruction of the Temple, that is to say, after the end of the fifth thousand (years since the Creation, according to the traditional Jewish calculations), which is all destruction, and a further two hundred years into the sixth thousand, and seventy years for the birthpangs, and two years for the birth itself, coming to the year 5272. But it is written: "Before (beterem) she was in labor, she brought forth" (Isaiah 66:7). And the secret of the matter is contained in the verse:"And it shall come to pass that before (terem) they call, I will answer" (Isaiah 65:24). And what is the meaning of this beterem (before)? The answer is that before (beterem) the completion of the seventy years and the two years following the passing of one thousand and two hundred years (from the beginning of the fifth thousand — tr.), where these seventy-two years are the birthpangs two Messiahs will be revealed to the world. And at that time:"And in His temple, all say:Glory." (Psalms 29:). And it has already been taught: "The wise shall inherit glory" (Proverbs 3:35). In other words: "And in His temple, all say: Glory, "the meaning of which is that the glory of the wise will be throughout His Temple.

702) And at that time, those Torah sages will be respected, those who suffered pangs and travails as a woman in labor, and who were despised by the simple folk, they will be honored. And immediately: "The Lord sat enthroned at the flood" (Psalms 29:10) on account of the wicked. Flood here symbolizes judgment, when "the fountains of the great deep and the windows of heaven were opened" (Genesis 7:11), as in the Flood. So, too, judgments will rise over them, over the wicked, above and below, with no end in sight for their judgments. And every contempt and disgrace shown by the idolatrous nations of the world towards God and His people — and how

many insults has Israel suffered from them for the sake of God's Name from all of them the Holy One, blessed be He, will exact vengeance, and therefore, as far as they are concerned, "The Lord avenges and is full of wrath" (Nahum 1:2).

THE FESTIVAL OF PASSOVER

703) "And in the first month" (Numbers 28:16). What is meant here by the first month? It is Nissan, which is when that being gave birth to the lights of the Redemption, in accord with the teaching of the sages of Mishnah: In the month of Nisan they were redeemed (from Egyptian bondage), and in the month of Nisan they will be redeemed (in the final Redemption). (Cf. Talmud Bavli, Rosh ha-Shanah 11a, top.) And this is with His hand, in the secret of the verse: "And he said: The hand upon the throne of the Lord" (Exodus 17:16), when He swore to remove the seed of Esau, the Amelikites from the world (see ibid. vol.14). At that time: "Draw out, and take lambs according to your families, and kill the passover lamb" (Exodus 12:21), where the meaning of 'draw out' [Hebrew root: mem shin kaph] is as in the verse: "He stretched out [Hebrew root: mem shin kaph] his hand with scorners" (Hosea 7:5).

704) At that time, thus said to the Lord to "the rulers who transgressed against Me (cf. Jeremiah 2:8): "Neither shall they enter into the land of Israel" (Ezekiel 13:9), and this refers to the leaders of the flock, the rulers of the generation. Wherefore it is said about them: "Therefore, behold, I will allure her and bring her into the wilderness" (Hosea 2:16). "And I will plead with you... as I pleaded with your fathers" (Ezekiel 20:35-36), i.e. whom He killed in the plague of darkness.

705) "And in the first month" (Numbers 28:16). What is meant

by the first month? This is the month in which that being, i.e. Malkhut, is revealed and strengthened and goes forth into the world, i.e. emerges from its closure, in the secret of the verse: "And strip the forests bare" (Psalms 29:9) (as above, 700) in 14 days. In 14 days refers to the remaining beings, i.e. Hesed and Gevurah, Tipheret and Malkhut, of Ze'ir Anpin, that illuminate within Malkhut, for they are ten in each direction, since Hesed and Gevurah, Tipheret and Malkhut, are the four directions in the four corners of the compass, north, south, east and west, each one of which is composed of ten Sephirot; and in the early writing it is stated that it, Malkhut, is Yod (ten), and that one Sephirah of Hesed and Gevurah, Tipheret and Malkhut, is in each of the four directions of the world, making fourteen. And since these four Hesed and Gevurah, Tipheret and Malkhut, join in and are corrected with the ten that are in Malkhut from the right-hand side, this makes "the fourteenth day of the month" (Numbers 28:16) for the correction of this being, which is Malkhut, with all its corrections, with rejoicing.

706) Rabbi Elazar said: Of course, that is how it is, but come and see: It is written: "Draw out and take lambs according to your families, and kill the passover lamb" (Exodus 12:21). What is the meaning of "draw out?" It is to be understood as one who draws something from that place to this, i.e. the upper days, which are the Sephirot of Ze'ir Anpin, to the lower days, to the Sephirot of Malkhut. The upper days of Ze'ir Anpin number 366, as in the numerical value of "draw out" [mishkhu: mem shin kaph waw, $40 + 300 + 20 + 6 = 366$], i.e. the number of days in a solar year, which is Ze'ir Anpin. The lower days of Malkhut are usually 354 days in a year, but when the moon, which is Malkhut, shines at its fullest, the number of its days rises to be 365 days, as the solar year, which is Ze'ir Anpin, i.e. as the numerical value of "Draw out" [mishkhu], less one.

707) Draw the upper days of Ze'ir Anpin to the lower days of Malkhut, so that they will be one, all joined together. And who draws them? That is, these ten of Malkhut when it is on the right hand side, that is Hesed? For it is written: "Be'asor (On the tenth day)" (Exodus 12:3), i.e. Malkhut, when on the right side. And there is a question to be asked here: Written is Be'asor (On the tenth day), when Scripture should have said Be'asarah (On the tenth day). [This is a stylistic point; the meanings are the same. — tr.] What is Be'asor (on the tenth day)? The answer to this is that there are nine in each direction with one point that goes in the middle, thus: ⚬ , and this point completes the ten Sephirot. This is why it is written: Be'asor (on the tenth day) (Exodus 12:3), just as it is written: Zakhor (Remember) (Exodus 20:8) and Shamor (Observe) (Deuteronomy 5:12), i.e. the form of the infinitive absolute of the verb, the meaning of Be'asor thus being to use the ten in such a way that these nine days will serve this point. "Of this month" (Exodus 12:3), which is Nisan, alludes to Hesed, to show that these days that are drawn down will be on the right side, which is Hesed, in order to combine zot [this, feminine form — tr.], which is Malkhut, with zeh [this, masculine form — tr.], which is Ze'ir Anpin, for it all to be one.

708) And when these four days that follow the tenth of the month join up with the four directions, north, south, east and west, which are the secret of Hesed and Gevurah, Tipheret and Malkhut, and combine with them, with the ten days, then that being, which is Malkhut, gives birth to the lights of the Redemption (as above, 706), and the Serpent departs. And at that time that being is sanctified on high, and is called "Glory," and then the festival is sanctified. This had not been the case previously, but now, in the festival, it is called "glory," as it is written: "And in His temple, all say: Glory" (Psalms 29:9) (as above, 700).

THE FAITHFUL SHEPHERD

709) The Faithful Shepherd said: These matters that are stated above, in the preceding paragraph, are insufficiently clear and they have to be explained for the companions, for whoever hides the secrets of the Torah from them, saddens them, for the lights of the secrets are darkness for the wicked. And such a one is like silver that is hidden away. If one digs until he discovers it, but it is not his, it becomes like darkness and gloom in his mind, while for one to whom it belongs, it illuminates for him. This is the reason why a person should reveal the hidden secrets of the Torah to the companions.

710) "In the tenth day" (Exodus 12:3) this means that the nine Sephirot are in all directions, paralleling the nine months of a pregnant woman's period of gestation, which is the same as the numerical value of ach [aleph chet] in one [echad: aleph chet dalet]. Who is the woman with child? She is the dalet in echad. Ach [aleph chet, 1 + 8 = 9] is the nine Sephirot in the four directions of the letter dalet [whose numerical value is four — tr.], and they are forty. Ach corresponds to "Remember" (Exodus 20:8), which is Ze'ir Anpin, while dalet corresponds to "Observe" (Deuteronomy 5:12), which is Malkhut, and together with them, this is forty-two.

711) This leaves us with "glory" to expound, as it is said: "Blessed be the name of the glory of His kingdom forever and ever" (inserted in the recital of the Shema Israel, after the first verse, Deuteronomy 6:4). And this is glory [kavod: kaph beit waw dalet, 20 + 2 + 6 + 4 = 32] and heart [lev: lamed beit, 30 + 2 = 32], the sum value of which is 64. And there are four times in each of the four directions of the dalet, that is 64 in four directions, which comes to 256 (as above, 339). And it has been taught: Glory above and heart below, and for this reason, the

recital of the unity (Shema Israel) is said twice daily, so that we thereby say 'glory' twice (in the response: Blessed be the name of the glory of His kingdom forever and ever), and glory twice produces the numerical sum of 64. Add to this the two dalets (of echad, one, in the Shema Israel, once in the morning and again in the evening, the numerical value of dalet being 4), and we have 64 + 4 + 4 = 72! And so the dalet of one (echad: aleph chet dalet) completes the 42-letter Name and also completes the 72-letter Name. And this is why it is said in A Psalm of David (Psalm 24): "Who is the King of glory? The Lord strong and mighty, the Lord mighty in battle" (v.8), and again: "Who then is the King of glory? The Lord of hosts, He is the King of glory" (v.10).

COMMENTARY

There are two unities, an upper unity and a lower unity, as was explained above (In the Introduction to the Sepher ha-Zohar, 204- 208, and in the commentary there, which should be studied). The upper unity is: "Let the waters (under the heaven) be gathered together into one place, and let the dry land appear" (Genesis 1:9), the meaning of which is: Let the stages that are under the heavens come together to be complete in six stages, which is the secret of the aleph chet of one (echad:aleph chet dalet). "And let the dryland appear" — That is, to connect these stages of Ze'ir Anpin that have been revealed to the dalet of echad that is called dry land, when it is from the chest and upwards, for it is there blocked off and all its lights are frozen. And this unity is the secret of the unity of the six words of the Shema Israel, namely: Hear, O-Israel, the-Lord, our God, the Lord, is-one, and this reveals hasadim to Ze'ir Anpin. But the dalet of echad has not yet received its correction, so that the Hokhmah that is in it will be able to illuminate, nor does it do so until the lower unity is effected, this being the secret of: "Let the earth put forth grass" (Genesis 1:11). And the unity is effected with "Blessed be the name of the glory of His kingdom forever and ever." And then what had been dry land, from the chest and upwards of Ze'ir Anpin, in the upper unity, when it now descends to be from the chest and below at "Blessed be the name of the glory of His kingdom forever and ever," becomes fruit — and herb-producing earth, since from the chest and downwards is revealed Hokhmah that is in the dalet of echad, and all the Sephirot of Ze'ir Anpin, which are aleph chet of echad, illuminate in their fullness in all the directions of the dalet of echad. (See there and also in the Commentator's Interpolation, par.5-9.)

And on the text (710): "The nine Sephirot are in all directions, paralleling the nine months of a pregnant woman's period of gestation, which is the same as the numerical value of ach (aleph chet) in one (echad: aleph chet dalet)." That is, in the upper unity of the Shema Israel, the dalet of echad receives from the nine Sephirot of Ze'ir Anpin, this being the secret of aleph chet (1 + 8 = 9), in the aspect of impregnating, which is the secret of nine months, nine Sephirot. "Who is the woman with child? She is the dalet in echad." That is to say: after the lower unity that is from the chest and downwards has been effected with "Blessed be the name of the glory of His kingdom forever and ever," she then gives birth to nine Sephirot, which is to say that they are revealed in her. But in the upper unity, the nine Sephirot of Ze'ir Anpin, which are the aleph chet of echad, are still covered and concealed in her as though as yet unborn. For then she is in the aspect of dry land, as above. And on the text: "Ach corresponds to...this is forty-two." This alludes to the 42-letter Name, for from the

chest and upwards of Ze'ir Anpin, which is where the upper
unity is, the 42-letter Name, with which the lights of Hokhmah
are covered, is in control. And after this upper unity has been
made, in the secret of the 42-letter Name, what remains is to
unite the lower unity of from the chest and downwards of
Ze'ir Anpin, in the secret of "Blessed be the name of the glory
of His kingdom forever and ever". And on the text (711): "This
leaves us with 'glory' to expound, as it is said: 'Blessed be the
name of the glory of His kingdom forever and ever:" That is, it
remains for us now to unite this lower unity, so that the dalet
of echad will give birth and reveal the nine Sephirot that it
receives in each of its sides on the upper unity. And on the
text: "And this is glory... and heart...," which is called glory in
which are revealed the 32 [= 30 + 2, lamed-beit, lev, heart]
paths of Hokhmah. And four times (64) comes to 256, alluding
to the secret of the 256 wings of the celestial beings. "And it
has been taught: Glory above and heart below." For above the
chest, Malkhut is called glory, but the revelation of the glory,
which is the 32 (numerical value of lev, heart) paths of
Hokhmah that are revealed by Malkhut, is only from the chest
and downwards of Ze'ir Anpin, in the unity of "Blessed be the
name of the glory of His kingdom forever and ever." And on
the text: "And for this reason the recital of the... Shema Israel
is said twice daily... "and we have 72! For the 72-letter Name,
which iş the Name of Names, is alluded at in the lower unity,
for in it Hokhmah is revealed. "So the dalet of one [echad:
aleph chet dalet] completes the 42-letter Name and also
completes the 72-letter Name." That is, the completion of the
upper mating that is from the chest and upwards for the
control of hasadim, which is the secret of the 42-letter Name;
and the completion of the illumination of Hokhmah that is
from the chest and downwards, which is the secret of the
72-letter Name. And this latter is derived from the three
verses: "And the angel of the Lord, who went before the camp

of Israel, removed and went behind them; and the pillar of cloud removed from them, and stood behind them; and it came between the camp of Egypt and the camp of Israel; and there was the cloud and the darkness here, yet gave it light by night there; and the one came not near to the other all the night. And Moses stretched out his hand over the sea; and the Lord caused the sea to go back by a strong east wind all the night, and made the sea dry land, and the waters were divided" (Exodus 14:19-21) [Each of these verses in Hebrew contains exactly 72 letters.] (See above, Beshallach, 173.) And on the text: "'Who is the King of glory? The Lord strong and mighty, the Lord mighty in battle,' and again: 'Who then is the King of glory? The Lord of hosts, He is the King of glory.'" (Psalms 24:8 and 10): That is, glory above and heart below, where the first King of glory is above the chest, where Malkhut is called glory in the secret of the 42-letter Name, and where the 32 paths of Hokhmah have no revelation. The second King of glory, about whom it is written "The Lord of hosts, He is the King of glory" (Psalms 24:10), is the glory that is below the chest, which is the secret of the 72-letter Name, where Hokhmah does have revelation.

712) It is written: "And in His temple, all say: Glory" (Psalms 29:9). What is meant by "in His temple?" This refers to the inner upper temple, where everything, i.e. Binah, is sanctified. There whoever is fitting for sanctification is sanctified. How is that temple sanctified? The answer to this is that initially the gates are opened by Da'at, which is Ze'ir Anpin, who ascends to Binah when the left side is in control of Binah, and becomes there the central column, which is the secret of Da'at that unites the right side and the left side, namely, Hokhmah and Binah, with each other, and opens the gates of Binah, i.e. opens

up Binah from its closure of the left. Thereby Ze'ir Anpin also receives from it three columns since three issue from one and one exists in three (as above, Bereshit Aleph, page 287), and this is further explained as follows: One concealed key, i.e. da'at, ordained and opened one gate on the south side, which is the secret of the right-hand column. Then the High Priest, which is the secret of Hesed, entered into that opening and stimulated with his girdle, which is the secret of Malkhut, and with his corrections, i.e. the four garments of an ordinary priest, namely, mitre, girdle, tunic, and breeches, which correspond to the four letters of 'The Lord' (aleph dalet nun yod), which is malkhut. Subsequently, he is adorned with a diadem of holiness, and puts on a breastplate and ephod and a robe of 70 bells and pomegranates, which are "gold bell and pomegranate," (Exodus 28:34) these being the secret of the intelligences of the illumination of Hokhmah that are drawn down from the first hey of the Tetragrammaton (Yod hey waw and hey), as above. And "the plate of the holy crown" (Exodus 39:30) on his forehead (Exodus 28:38), is called the plate of the holy crown,i.e. the yod of the Tetragrammaton (yod hey waw and hey). And he was embellished with the four garments of gold and with the four garments of white, which correspond to the eight letters in the names of the Tetragrammaton (yod hey waw and hey) and 'The Lord' (aleph dalet nun yod), and on that plate 42 letters sparkle, i.e. the 42-letter Name (as above, 711), and the whole of that palace shines with upper lights.

713) And that key, which is the secret of Da'at, as above, turned and opened another side of Binah, to the north. Then Levi, which is the secret of Gevurah and the left hand column, entered, and he is the tithe of Jacob, whom he set aside for the Holy One, blessed be He, and with him the ten-stringed lyre, which is the secret of the ten Sephirot of the left column. And he was crowned with his diadems, i.e. the intelligences of

the upper three Sephirot who are called diadems. And then the key turned yet again and opened another gate of that temple, that gate that stands in the center, i.e. the column that is on eastern side, which is Tipheret, the central column. He enters, i.e. Tipheret, and is adorned in that gate with seventy diadems, which are the secret of the 72-letter Name. And he is adorned with four letters, which are twelve, i.e. with the twelve possible combinations of the four letters of the Tetragrammaton (yod hey waw and hey) (which are:1) yod hey waw and hey; 2) yod hey hey waw; 3) yod waw hey hey;4) hey waw hey yod; 5) hey waw yod hey; 6) hey hey waw yod; 7) waw hey yod hey; 8) waw hey hey yod; 9) waw yod hey hey; 10) hey yod hey waw; 11) hey yod waw hey; 12) hey hey yod waw). And these are the secrets of Hesed and Gevurah, Tipheret and Malkhut, in each of the three columns. And he was adorned with the inscriptions of the two hundred and seventy thousand worlds, i.e. the place where the illumination of Hokhmah is revealed, which is from the chest and downward, where the illumination of Hokhmah is termed a thousand, and there are two thirds of Tipheret which are seventy, and Netsach and Hod, in each one of which there are ten Sephirot, making two hundred and seventy Sephirot. And he is embellished with crowns that shine from one end of the world to the, i.e. the Malkhut that is called world, and a number of valuable garments and a number of holy crowns.

714) That key, which is Da'at, as above, turned once again and opened all the concealed gates and all the hidden holy gates, and Ze'ir Anpin was sanctified in them, and stands there as King. That is, in the aspect of Malkhut which is in the central column of Binah, He is there blessed with a number of blessings and crowned with a number of crowns. Then all of them issue forth from Binah to their places in Ze'ir Anpin, i.e. Hokhmah and Binah of Ze'ir Anpin from the two gates to the south and north of Binah; and the half-right of Da'at, from the

central gate of Binah, and half of Da'ats left, and all of them issue forth, joined together, and are crowned with their diadems as is fitting. Once they have left Binah for the places of Ze'ir Anpin, they awaken Ze'ir Anpin so that He will put on His adornments, i.e. the four intelligences as above.

715) And this being,i.e. Malkhut, which is in the first state and still cleaves to the left, awakens and contracts itself out off love of the song, i.e. because of the longing for hasadim, for since it is on the left without the right, it has Hokhmah without hasadim, something that causes it great distress, and it longs deeply for hasadim, which is why it contracted itself into the aspect of below the chest, so that it should be able to receive hasadim from His. (As above, Bereshit Aleph, 110-115) And how does it contract itself? Out of love of the song it contracts itself bit by bit until it becomes just a point, under Yesod from the aspect of the lights, while from the aspect of the tools it is a point under the chest. And since she has contracted herself, it is then written: "And there went a man of the house of Levi" (Exodus 2:1), which is the secret of the Holy One, blessed be he: "And he took a wife, a daughter of Levi" (ibid.), which is Malkhut. It is certainly called a daughter of Levi, because it is from the left side. How does he take her? He puts his left hand under her head, out of love, i.e. the left side of Ze'ir Anpin becomes the upper three Sephirot of Malkhut, and are referred to as head, this being in the secret of the verse: "His left hand under my head" (Song of Songs, 8:3.)

716) And you might well ask that, since Malkhut is now a small point, how could Ze'ir Anpin unite with a small point? The answer is that vis-a-vis above, the smaller a thing is the more praiseworthy it is, and this is a virtue, but it is really supremely large, for, when it is small, the High Priest

immediately awakens for her, the referrence being to Hesed of Ze'ir Anpin who holds and embraces her. Had Malkhut been large, she would not have been able to unite at all, but, since she contracted herself and is a small point, the Sephiort of Ze'ir Anpin can hold her, and raise her up on high, between the two arms of Ze'ior Anpin,namely, Hesed and Gevurah. And after they have raised her up, she sits between these two sides, namely Hesed and Gevurah, and then the column that stands in the center,i.e.Tipheret, which is the central column, joins with her in a sensual love, a love of perfect union. And then: "And Jacob", that is, Ze'ir Anpin, "kissed Rachel," who is Malkhut (Genesis 29:11), for with the love of kisses, they cleave to each other without separation, until she receives a soul (nephesh) of delights as is fitting.

COMMENTARY

So long as Malkhut is in the first state,i.e. in the secret of the two great lights (cf.Genesis 1:16), when both of them receive from Binah (for Ze'ir Anpin enclothes the right column of Binah, which is hasadim and Malkhut enclothes the left column of Binah which is Hokhmah) Malkhut has no desire to unite with Ze'ir Anpin nor to receive hasadim from him, and she is as distant from him as the left hand is from the right. And in order to receive hasadim from Ze'ir Anpin, she had to contract herself into a point below Yesod of Ze'ir Anpin, i.e. to the lowest level under Ze'ir Anpin,and she is no longer able to receive from Binah, but only from Ze'ir Anpin , who is above her. And therefore then, when she is a point under him she unites with him as one, and receives from him all the intelligences of greatness (all of which is clarified in Bereshit Aleph, 110-115),q.v) And on the text: "The smaller a thing is the more praiseworthy it is...and had she been large...[they]

would not have been able to unite at all:" For so long as Malkhut was as large as Ze'ir Anpin, they were unable to unite, but Malkhut was dispute with him, as the right-hand column and left-hand column before they were united by the central column (as above in the Idra Rabba,214). "But, since she contracted herself...;" for she then unites with Ze'ir Anpin with kisses and copulation, and receives from him all the greatness.

717) When she receives a soul (nephesh) of delights, as is fitting, and she wants to visit her hosts, they all gather together and call her: Glory, glory, glory from the holy temple of Father and Mother; and in the holy temple itself, Father and Mother, i.e. Hokhmah and Binah, open by saying: Sanctified, sanctified! In other words they emanate to Malkhut from their lights which are called holiness. Then the month, which is Malkhut, is sanctified properly. And it is then written: "And in the first month" (Numbers 28:16), for it is certainly the first. And this is because previously, when Malkhut was attached to the left column without the right, she was not considered to be in existence because her lights were blocked up and she was unable to emanate, but now, having contracted to a point and been rebuilt by Father and Mother in the lights of holiness, and being under the level of Ze'ir Anpin, she is considered to be in her first existence, and it is therefore then written about her: "And in the first month" (ibid.). And therefore, Scripture says: "Draw out and take lambs..."(Exodus 12:21), the meaning of which is: Draw down the upper days of Ze'ir Anpin to Malkhut (as above, 706), and it is therefore written: "In the tenth day of this month" (Exodus 12:3), the meaning of which is that the Moon, which is Malkhut, has become joined to the Sun, which is Ze'ir Anpin, i.e. that the nine Sephirot of Ze'ir Anpin will serve to illuminate Malkhut (as above,707). And

whereas she was a single point after the contraction, when she
descended from the temple of Father and Mother, she now
expands bit by bit and fills out and becomes the final hey of
the Tetragrammaton (yod hey waw and hey), which is full of
emanation from all four directions and is properly sanctified.

THE FAITHFUL SHEPHERD

718) (The beginning of this section is omitted.) That temple
turned and opened another gate on the south side, i.e. in the
right-hand column, with 72 crowns, which is the secret of the
72-letter Name that illuminates in the right-hand column, and
later it opens a third gate on the eastern side, which is the
central column, with fifty lights, of the fifty gates of Binah.
Next it opens another gate on the western side, which is the
secret of Malkhut in the 72 crowns of the 72-letter Name, and
all the 248 hasadim, 248 being the number of words in the
sections of the recital of the Shema Israel. And whereas this
celestial being, which is Malkhut, was initially small, at that
time, having received 72 crowns and 248 hasadim, she grows,
which is as is written: "The whole Earth is full of His glory"
(Isaiah 6:3), which is the upper glory and the lower glory, all
of which Malkhut receives with the declaration of the unity in
the recital of the Shema Israel (as Above, 711, q.v.).

719) When he reaches the Life (chay: chet yod, 8 + 10 = 18) of
the Worlds, in which are the 18 blessings of the prayer, i.e. in
the shemoneh esreh prayer, which he starts with "O Lord, open
my lips, and my mouth shall declare Your praise" (Psalms
51:17), then the central column, which is Ze'ir anpin, joins
with her with affectionate kisses of the lips, which are Netsach
and Hod; and tongue, which is the Righteous One, that is
Yesod, is between them is the secret of the language of

study. At that time; "And Jacob kissed Rachel" (Genesis 29:11), where Jacob is Ze'ir Anpin and Rachel is Malkhut, and then that celestial being, Malkhut, is called Glory, glory and Father and Mother say Sanctified, sanctified. That is, Father and Mother emanate to her their lights that are called holiness (as above, 717), and then the month, which is Malkhut, is correctly sanctified. And she is then called"And in the first month" (Numbers 28:16),first without a doubt (as is explained there).

720) And then: "Draw out" (Exodus 12:21) the upper days of Ze'ir Anpin to Malkhut (as above, 706), which is why it is written: "In the tenth day of this month" (ibid. v.3), the meaning of which is that the nine Sephirot of Ze'ir Anpin shine towards Malkhut (as above, 707), i.e. that the holy moon, which is Malkhut, is joined to the sun, which is Ze'ir Anpin, about which it is said: "For the Lord God is a sun and a shield" (Psalms 84:12). And whereas Malkhut was a small point, she filled out as the full moon, and then the month is full, i.e.the moon, which is Malkhut, is full, and "The whole earth is full of His glory" (Isaiah 6:3). Initially she was lacking, but now she is complete, full.

721) Rabbi Hiyya began by quoting: "On the fourteenth day of the month is the passover" (Numbers 28:16). Why is the paschal sacrifice a lamb? The answer to this is that the Egyptians worshipped the lamb which was one of their gods, for they worshipped the constellation Aries (which is symbolized by a ram- tr.)(cf. Midrash Shemot Rabba 17,3). Come and See: It is written:"For we shall sacrifice the abomination of the Egyptians" (Exodus 8:22). What is meant by "the abomination of the Egyptians?" Could it be that because it is hateful to them it is called "the abomination of the Egyptians?" On the contrary, it is called "the abomination of the Egyptians" because it is the Egyptians idol and their god. it is similarly written: "The

abomination of the nations" (Deuteronomy 18:9), the meaning of which is the idolatry of the nations.

722) Come and see the wisdom of Joseph, as is written: "And from among his brethren he took five men" (Genesis 47:2), and he taught them to say: "Your servants are shepherds" (ibid. v.3). And would a king who was ruler over the country and who was like a father to Pharaoh have done such a thing to his brothers to make the Egyptians hate them and not show them consideration? For if you hold the view that the abomination of the Egyptians is every shepherd, which means hated by the Egyptians, then this would be the implication of what Joseph did. But in reality the abomination of the Egyptians is what their idol and their god was called. Therefore is it written: "For we shall sacrifice the abomination of the Egyptians" (Exodus 8:22).

723) Joseph said; All the best of Egypt, the land of Raamses (cf. Genesis 47:11), and this part of the country they set aside for their god, i.e. the flocks, for them to be pastured and go there to their hearts' delight. And all the Egyptians considered those who tended their gods as themselves gods. Thus Joseph said: I shall arrange it so that my brothers inherit that country, and the Egyptians shall bow down to them, and will accord them proper treatment, and this is what is written: "for every shepherd is an abomination to the Egyptians" (Genesis 47:34). Which is to say that, for this reason, they (the Egyptians) should treat them (Joseph's bothers) as their (the Egyptians') gods.

724) Rabbi Yossi said: Just as the Holy One, blessed be He, punishes idolaters, so will He punish idolatry (cf. Talmud Yerushalmi, Hagigah, 2, 5). If this is so, why did Joseph make his bothers into idols, that the Egyptians should bow down to

them as though they were gods (as above). He replied to him: Joseph did not make his brothers into idols but into rulers over the idolatry of the Egyptians, and thus subdued their idolatry under the hand of his brothers, so that they (the brothers) would smite it (the idolatry) with the rod. Joseph said: If my bothers control their (the Egyptians') idolatry, then how much better will they have rule over (the Egyptians) themselves, which is why he settled them in the best of the country and made them rulers over all the land.

725) And so, to return to the question that was asked above (721): Why is the paschal sacrifice a lamb? The answer is because a lamb was the idol and god of the Egyptians. Said the Holy One, blessed be He: From the tenth of the month, take the god of the Egyptians, and bind it and let it be imprisoned and hold it in your keeping one day, and two, and three days, and on the fourth day do to it what has to be done, and assemble over it.

726) And when the Egyptians heard the voice of their idol which was being held by Israel, and they were unable to rescue it, they cried and it was as difficult for them as though they themselves had been tied up for the kill. Said the Holy One, blessed be He: Let it be tied up in your possession day after day for four days, so that the Egyptians may see it when it is caught, and on the fourth day, bring it out to be killed and let the Egyptians see how you enact judgment on it. And this, i.e. these judgments that they (Israel) performed on their (the Egyptians') idol, were harder for them to bear than all the plagues that the Holy One, blessed be He, brought on them.

727) Subsequently, they cast it into the fire, as it is written: "And the images of their gods you shall burn with fire" (Cf. Deuteronomy 7:5). Said the Holy One, blessed be He: "Do not

eat of it raw" (Exodus 12:9) so that the Egyptians will not say: They were so desirous of and had such a longing for our god that they ate it insufficiently roasted. It was decreed that it should be eaten roasted and not boiled, for had it been boiled it would have been covered under the water in the pan, and they (the Egyptians) would not have seen it, but its correction is that they (the Egyptians) should see it when it is being burnt in the fire, since its odor then spreads far and wide.

728) Moreover, its head and its legs were to be with it (cf. ibid.) so that they (the Egyptians) should not say that it was some animal or other thing, but that they should recognize it as their god. Moreover, it was not to be eaten out of hunger, but on a full stomach (cf. Tosephta, Pesachin 5, 3) by way of disgrace and contempt. Moreover, "neither shall you break a bone thereof" (Exodus 12:46), but they (the Egyptians) should see its bones cast into the market-place and be unable to rescue it. For this reason it is written: "Upon their gods the Lord executed judgments" (Numbers 33:4), that is, many judgments. Moreover, "and your staff is your hand" (Exodus 12:11), but not a sword, spear, nor any other instrument of war, in order to demonstrate that you (Israel) are not afraid of them (the Egyptians).

729) Rabbi Yehudah said: We have already learned that the Egyptians worshipped the constellation of Aries, which is why they worshipped the lamb. Rabbi Yossi said: If that is so, they should have worshipped a ram (which is the symbol of Aries), a baby ram, rather than a lamb (which is a baby sheep). He answered him: They worshipped them all. The constellation of Aries ascends and descends, sometimes appearing as a ram and at others like a large lamb, for which reason they worshipped them all. He said to him: What I have heard is that every large animal was a god for them, which is why the Holy One,

blessed be He, killed all the first-born of the cattle (see Exodus
12:29). And we have already learned that these were the stages
on high: i.e. upper spiritual forces of impurity were called
first-born of cattle, and that was why they worshipped them.

730) Rabbi Elazar said: It is written: "You shall eat nothing
leavened" (Exodus 12:20), and it is written: "There shall no
leavened bread be eaten" (Exodus 13:3). What is the difference
between these two: nothing leavened [machmetset] and no
leavened bread [chamets]? The latter is masculine, while the
former is feminine. Rabbi Shimeon said: Elazar, my son, in the
former case it is written "you shall eat no," while in the latter
case it is written "it shall not be eaten." Why in the latter case,
does it not say: You shall eat no leavened bread (on a parallel
with the former verse: You shall eat nothing leavened)? The
answer to this is that, with the female, who is more inclined to
corrupt her ways, the statement is by way of warning: You
shall not eat, but in the case of the male of the shells, who is
more inclined to grasp a thread of purity than the female, the
statement is by way of request: It shall not be eaten, which is
not the language of warning or command. This is why it is
written in the one case (Exodus 13:3) "It shall not be eaten,"
and in the other case (ibid, 12:20) "You shall not eat."

731) He said to him: But father, it is also written: "You shall
eat no leavened bread with it" (Deuteronomy 16:3), i.e. the
language of warning is also used for chamets, which is the male
of a shell. He replied: In honor of the sacrifice, Scripture uses
many extra words, and therefore says: "You shall eat no
leavened bread with it" (ibid.), but initially it was said about
chamets: "It shall not be eaten" (Exodus 13:3), which is the
language of request. But subsequently, about machmetset, a
warning is used: "You shall not eat" (Exodus 12:20), for the
female of the shells is the most difficult of the two of them, of

the male and female of the shells. What is the reason for machmetset being so called? It is because there is a smell of death there. Chamets alludes to the male and has therefore no allusion to death, but machmetset is female. And it is written: "Her feet go down to death" (Proverbs 5:5). Thus, the first and last letters of the word machmetset [mem chet mem tsade tav] are mem and tav that spell dead [met: mem tav]. Thus she, the female, greets anyone who eats leavened bread on passover with death, and it should be known that he dies in this world and in the world to come, as it is written: "Whosoever eats that which is leavened, that soul shall be cut off from the congregation of Israel" (Exodus 12:19).

732) Why is the unleavened bread called matsah (see Exodus 12:8)? It is as we have learned concerning the verse "I am God Almighty" (Genesis 35:11), the word for Almighty being Shaddai, which is interpreted as meaning "I am the one who [she-] said to His world Enough [day]" (cf. Talmud Bavli, Hagigah 12a); i.e. May He who said to His world Enough, say to our troubles Enough, i.e. may He chase away from us the judgments and troubles. Matsah (unleavened bread) is likewise, for it subdues and subjugates; i.e. it scatters the evil ones to all sides and makes a quarrel with them, just as the Name Shaddai ('Almighty,' which is inscribed on the outside of the case) of the mezuzah chases away the shades and demons that are at the entrance. So, too, matsah chases them away from all the dwellings of holiness, and makes a quarrel and a fight with them, as it is written: "Massah and Meribah" (Exodus 17:7), where Massah [mem samekh hey] means trying and Meribah means a quarrel, and therefore the name is written: matsah [mem tsade hey]. But this has to be queried since massah is written with a samekh, and not with a tsade, as is matsah. The answer to this is that the (Aramaic) translation of massah is matsuta [mem tsade waw tav aleph], i.e. with the letter tsade,

the samekh and the tsade being thus interchangeable here, and
therefore matsah (unleavened bread) is written [as equivalent to
massah, trying — tr.]

THE FAITHFUL SHEPHERD

733) The Faithful Shepherd said: Just as the tongue is a rod
over all members of the household (and cf. 724), for he
chastises them with his tongue, which is the same for them as
though he has chastised them with a rod; and as the tongue is
the secret of the letter waw, which is Ze'ir Anpin that is called
the Tetragrammaton [yod hey waw and hey], and is cane or rod
in which are ten letters; for the Tetragrammaton, when written
out and filled in with alephs, has ten letters — yod waw dalet
hey aleph waw aleph waw hey aleph — and with it the Holy
One, blessed be He, smote (the Egyptians) with ten plagues
through him (Moses); and since all the plagues were from the
side of the hey of the Tetragrammaton [yod hey waw and hey],
therefore Rabbi Akiva says: How do we know that each plague
that the Holy One, blessed be He, brought down on the
Egyptians in Egypt consisted of five plagues? (Cf. e.g.
Mekhilta, Beshallach, 6 and the Passover Haggadah.) We should
deduce from this that... at the sea they were smitten with 250
plagues. And the letter hey (whose numerical value is 5) times
the letter yod (whose numerical value is 10) gives 50 plagues,
and hey (5) times 50 is 250, which is why at the sea they were
smitten with 250 plagues.

734) Joseph gave his brothers possession of all the best of the
land of Egypt, which is Raamses (cf. Genesis 47:11), and this is
the land that they set aside for their god to pasture and move
in to its heart's content. And all the Egyptians considered those
who tend their gods as themselves gods. And what Joseph

requested from Pharaoh (see Genesis 47:1) was the land of
Raamses to tend their flocks, in order to place his brothers in
control over the gods of Egypt, so that they should be
subjugated under them as slaves under their king, and that all
of them should be subjugated under the Name of Names, the
Tetragrammaton on their part, and that none should rule in the
world excepting the Name of Names, and that all the
subordinates to Him should also be subjugated.

735) And to show them that He will in the future punish
them, as it is written: "And against all the gods of Egypt I will
execute judgments" (Exodus 12:12), because they mislead
mankind and make themselves divine; and since the appointee
of the ram (Aries) is greater than the appointees of the other
gods, the Holy One, blessed be He, commanded Israel: "They
shall take to them every man a lamb, according to their fathers'
houses, a lamb for a household" (Exodus 12:3); and He gave
them (Israel) control over it (the Egyptian god), and they took
hold of it as they did for one day, and for two and three days,
and subsequently they brought it out for judgments in the eyes
of all Egypt, to demonstrate that their god is at Israel's disposal
to enact judgement on it.

736) Therefore is it written: "Eat not of it raw, nor sodden at
all with water, but roast with fire; its head with its legs and
with the inwards thereof" (Exodus 12:9), so that it should be
judged in the roasting fire, and He commanded that its bones
be cast wantonly into the market-place, wherefore is it written:
"Neither shall you break a bone thereof" (ibid. v. 46). And He
commanded that on the fourth day, after it had been bound for
three days, judgement be enacted upon it. And this was harder
for them (for the Egyptians to bear) than all the plagues with
which the Holy One, blessed be He, smote them through the
Faithful Shepherd (Moses).

Futhermore, He commanded that it not be eaten with appetite, but with a full stomach (cf. Tosephta, Pesachim 5, 3). And immediately on their seeing its bones in the market-place and being unable to rescue it, this was the most difficult thing for them. Furthermore, it is said about them: "And your staff in your hand" (ibid. v.11), to subdue all the gods of Egypt under your hand. And since their gods are the first-born of the angels, it is written: "And the Lord smote all the first-born" (ibid. v.29).

737)   And after all this, it is written: "No leavened bread shall be eaten; for seven days you shall eat with it unleavened bread [matsah], even the bread of affliction" (Deuteronomy 16:3). And it is written: "You shall eat nothing leavened" (Exodus 12:20). Said the Faithful Shepherd: Why did He command not to eat leavened bread for seven days, but to eat on them unleavened bread [matsah]? And why in one case is it written: "It shall not be eaten" (Deuteronomy 16:3), while in the other case it is written: "You shall not eat" (Exodus 12:20)? The answer is that there are seven planets, namely Saturn, Jupiter, Mars, Sun, Venus, Mercury, and Moon, and these are the secret of Hesed, Gevurah, Tipheret, Netsach, Hod, Yesod, and Malkhut, that are in the vessels of the rear of Malkhut. And they are from the side of good and evil, for the light that is at the front is matsah (unleavened bread), while the shell that is on the outside is chamets, (leavened bread). And the chamets (leavened bread) is masculine, while machmetset (anything leavened) is feminine, and they are male and female of that same shell that is on the outside. And about the male of the shell, which is not that serious, it is said: "It shall not be eaten" (Deuteronomy 16:3), but about the female of the shell, which is a serious matter, it is said: "You shall not eat" (Exodus 12:20) (as above, 730).

738)   The matzah that is within the seven above-mentioned

planets is 'guarded' from the shells, which are "the seven
maidens, who were meant to be given her out of the king's
house" (Esther 2:9), i.e. the vessels of the rear of Malkhut of
Atsilut, which Hokhmah is enclothed at the time of the growth
of Malkhut (as explained above, Vayaqhel, 53, which should be
well studied). And about them it is said: "And you shall
observe the feast of unleavened bread" (Exodus 12:17) [which is
taken here as meaning: And you shall guard the unleavened
bread, the matsot — tr.] Matsah is guarded, or preserved, from
the shells, for its husband, who is waw, i.e. Ze'ir Anpin, which
is the secret of the waw of the Tetragrammaton [yod hey waw
and hey]. And matsah [mem tsade hey, unleavened bread],
when a waw is added to it, becomes mitsvah [mem tsade waw
hey, a precept].

739) And he who guards it for the hidden yod hey in the mem
tsade of matsah [mem tsade hey], for, in the Atbash alphabet
[where the final letter of the alphabet, tav, is substituted for
the first letter, aleph, and the penultimate letter, shin, for the
second letter, beit, and so on — tr.], the mem of matsah is
replaced by yod, and the tsade of matsah is replace by hey, this
therefore being the secret of the hidden yod hey in the mem
tsade of matsah. And the Holy One, blessed be He, commanded
that Malkhut be blessed with seven blessings on the Eve of
Passover, namely, its seven maidens (see Esther 2:9), i.e. the
seven vessels Hesed, Gevurah, Tipheret, Netsach, Hod, Yesod,
and Malkhut of Atsilut, from the aspect of the rear, as above,
which are called Saturn, Jupiter, Mars, Sun, Venus, Mercury,
and Moon. And He commanded that the shells, which are
chamets (leavened bread) and machmetset (anything leavened)
be removed from them, for they are dark clouds that cover the
lights of the seven planets, as it is said about them: "And when
they had eaten them up, it could not be known that they had
eaten them; but they were still ill-favored," i.e. darkness, "as at

the beginning." (Genesis 41:21). For the darkness of their
clouds is so strong that the lights that are in the seven planets
are unable to illuminate, and for this reason: "It could not be
known that they had eaten them" (ibid.).

REBUKE THE WILD BEAST OF THE REEDS

740) Rabbi Shimeon said: "Rebuke the wild beast of the reeds,
the multitude of the bulls, with the calves of the peoples"
(Psalms 68:31). "The wild beast" is that beast on to which Esau
held. "Reeds" is, as we have learned, for on the day that
Solomon took the daughter of Pharaoh, Gabriel came and stuck
a reed in the sea, and a city, Rome was built on it. (Cf.
Talmud Bavli, Shabbat 56b.) What is "reed?" It is the male of
that wicked being onto which Esau held, which has a small
part in the unity of holiness, namely the reed that Gabriel
stuck into the great sea. And for this reason it controls the
world, and about this rule it is written: "The reeds and flags
shall wither" (Isaiah 19:6). "Reed" is the regime over all
kingdoms, and futhermore it is for this reason called "reed",
since in ʌhe future the Holy One, blessed be He, is going to
break ıt as this reed.

COMMENTARY:

Lillith and Samael are called "the wild beast of the reeds,"
which are the male and female of a shell, and Esau holds on to
them. And on the text: "Is that beast on to which Esau held,"
and the male of the shell is as in the middle between the
holiness and the shell, for the male, which is called 'reed,' is

attached to holy Malkhut, and the impure female that is called
'beast' is attached to it and is Hokhmah of the shell. And on
the text: "What is 'reed?' It is the male of that wicked being on
which Esau held, which has a small part in the unity of
holiness," for the male is attached to Malkhut of holiness. And
this is the reed "that Gabriel stuck into the great sea." The great
sea refers to Malkhut, and a reed, which is the male of the
shell, is stuck into it.

741) Come and see: In Egypt that "wild beast of the reeds"
rules, and a number of different types of regime issue from it.
And they all are in the secret of chamets (leavened bread).
Since the Holy One, blessed be He, broke it (the beast), He
removed the chamets (leavened bread) and introduced matsah
(unleavened bread). What did He use to break it? With the
smallest and thinnest thread, He broke the letter chet of
chamets [chet mem tsade], making it into the letter hey, thus
resulting in the letters hey mem tsade, which, when
re-arranged, spell matsah [mem tsade hey]. That is, He broke
the letter chet of this being called chamets. Thus it is called
"the wild beasts of the reeds" (Psalms 68:31) because it is as
easy to break as is this reed. With what was it broken? It was
with a thread small as a hair that He broke the chet and
removed it from its former state and it became matsah.
Therefore it is written: "Rebuke the wild beast of the reeds"
(Psalms 68:31), for the Holy One, blessed be He, rebuked it,
and the chet of chamets was broken and became a hey.

742) And in the future the Holy One, blessed be He, will
break that reed as follows: He will break off the foot of the
qoph of qaneh (reed), making it into a hey, and thus qaneh
[qoph nun hey] will become hineh [hey nun hey, behold], as is

written: "Behold, the Lord God will come as a Mighty One, and
His arm will rule for Him; Behold, His reward is with Him,
and His recompense before Him" (Isaiah 40:10). What is the
meaning of "and His recompense before Him?" This is the
recompense of that letter qoph, whose foot is broken off, and
this is recompense before Him, for He removes the foot of the
qoph of qaneh [qoph nun hey, reed], making it into hineh [hey
nun hey, behold]. "A harbinger unto Zion (will I give): Behold,
behold them" (Isaiah 41:27).

COMMENTARY:

"The wild beast of the reeds" (Psalms 68:31) is the secret of the
male and female of the shell, which are attached to the left
without the right and draw Hokhmah of the left down, from
above downwards, and with this the pipes of Malkhut come to
an end. For the reed, which is the secret of the male of the
shell, is attached to Malkhut, in the secret of 'He stuck a reed
in the great sea,' as above. And chamets (leavened bread) is the
secret of chayah (wild beast, being), i.e. the female of the shell.
And in order to open the pipes for the emanation that is in
Malkhut, it is necessary to break the reed and the wild beast of
the shell that cover the lights of Malkhut, i.e. to contract the
upper three Sephirot of the left side and prevent the wild beast
of the reeds from suckling from them, and they will be
separated from Malkhut, and then the pipes of the emanation
that are in Malkhut will be opened. And this is understood in
terms of foot? His breaking the foot of the letter chet of
chamets [chet mem tsade], which is the wild beast of the shell,
for the breaking of Netsach, Hod, and Yesod of the vessels
causes the disappearance of the upper three Sephirot of the

lights, and the chamets (unleavened bread) returns to be guarded matsah (leavened bread) for its owner/husband; i.e. the emanation of Hokhmah will not illuminate in it, but in the aspect of the six intermediate Sephirot of Hokhmah, i.e. from below upwards. For then the wild beast of the reeds is unable to suckle, and it is preserved for Ze'ir Anpin, its husband. And it is also understood in terms of the foot of the qoph of qaneh [qoph nun hey, reed], which is the male of the shell that is stuck into Malkhut, being broken. And thus from qaneh (reed) is derived hineh (behold), which is the secret of the verse: "Behold, His reward is with Him" (Isaiah 40:10), for following the breaking of the foot of the qoph, the reward of the righteous is revealed.

And this is what he says: He broke the letter chet of this being called chamets [chet mem tsade], i.e. He contracted the upper three Sephirot of the left side, thereby breaking the foot of the chet of chamets. However, this contraction can be achieved in one of the two ways. Either by a revelation of the Lock, which is Malkhut of the attribute of Judgement, which is a powerful force that contracts it also from the six intermediate Sephirot of Hokhmah, i.e. even from the drawing down of Hokhmah, upwards from below; Or it can be contracted by a revelation of the Key, when Hokhmah contracts only from the upper three Sephirot and remains in the six intermediate Sephirot, as has been explained above (Lekh, page 13, q.v.). And on the text: "With the smallest... thread, He broke the letter chet of chamets," i.e. with the Key, which is the smallest contraction, He broke the chet of chamets. And therefore it became matsah, for the letters of chamets [chet mem tsade, leavened bread] became matsah [mem tsade hey, unleavened bread], which is to say that the six intermediate Sephirot of Hokhmah, called matsah, remained in it. Since its contraction was not difficult from the point of view of the Lock, and together with

the breaking of the foot of the chet of chamets, which is the
female of the shell, the foot of the qoph of qaneh [qoph nun
hey] was also broken, this being the male of the shell. And on
the text: "He will break off the foot of the qoph of qaneh
(reed), making it into a hey, and thus qaneh [qoph nun hey]
will become hineh [hey nun hey, behold]." That is, the qaneh
(reed) will be separated from Malkhut, and Malkhut will be
left guarded alone, for Malkhut is called hineh (behold). And
on the text: "Behold, the Lord God will come as a Mighty One,
and His arm will rule for Him; Behold His reward is with Him,
and His recompense before Him" (Isaiah 40:10)." For following
the breaking of the qaneh (reed), and its separation from
Malkhut, the pipes of the emanation that are in Malkhut are
then opened, and the reward of the righteous is revealed, this
being the secret of: "Behold, His reward is with Him, and His
recompense before Him" (ibid.). The question is then put: What
is the meaning of "and His recompense before Him," to which
the answer is given: "This is the recompense of that letter qoph,
whose foot is broken off," for the breaking off of the foot of
the qoph is the secret of "and His recompense before Him," the
reward and the recompense for the contraction of the upper
three Sephirot come together. "And this is the recompense
before Him." That is to say that the upper three Sephirot are
called 'face' and the act of the contraction that is made in the
upper three Sephirot is grasped as an act/recompense before
Him (literally: in His face). Wherefore Scripture says: "And His
recompense before Him" (ibid.). And then the verse "A
harbinger unto Zion (will I give): Behold, behold them" (Isaiah
41:27) will be fulfilled.

THE FAITHFUL SHEPHERD

743) Rabbi Shimeon opened with the verse: "Rebuke the wild
beast of the reeds, the multitude of the bulls, with the calves

of the peoples" (Psalms 68:31). "Rebuke the wild beast of the reeds" refers to a reed (to which is attached Esau, which is a large city, Rome) that Gabriel stuck as a reed in the great sea-which is a secret, for the reed is attached to Malkhut that is called the great sea, and on it a large city, Rome was built, which is the secret of the kingdom of Esau. And this is a reed that is called chamets (leavened bread). When the Redemption comes to Israel, He will break that reed, as it is written: "Rebuke the wild beast of the reeds, the multitude" (ibid.), and the chamets that is drawn down from the reed is immediately removed from the world, with its machmetset, i.e. its female, which is a Rome, and matsah (unleavened bread) will be revealed in the world, for this is the Temple, the First Temple and the Second Temple, which are Binah and Malkhut.

744) The Faithful Shepherd said: They, the First Temple and the Second Temple, correspond to the pupil of the right eye and the pupil of the left eye, and they correspond to the large and small (city) Rome, paralleling the two eyelids that cover the pupils of the right eye and of the left eye, and they, in turn, correspond to leaven and leavened bread. And so long as these are not removed from the world, with not one of them being seen or found, the First Temple and the Second Temple are unable to be revealed in the world.

745) And what healing will there be for the eyelids that darken the pupils of the right and left eyes? This is the gall of a calf, as it is written: "There shall the calf feed and there shall he lie down" (Isaiah 27:10). "There shall be calf feed" refers to the Messiah son of Joseph, about whom it is said: "His firstling bullock, majesty is his" (Deuteronomy 33:17), which is the secret of the face of ox from the left side. "And there shall he lie down" refers to the Messiah son of David. One, namely, Messiah son of David, removes the large (city) Rome, and the

other, namely Messiah son of Joseph, removes the small (city)
Rome; and corresponding to them are Michael and Gabriel,
where the former corresponds to Messiah son of David and the
latter to Messiah son of Joseph.

COMMENTARY:

The large and small (cities) Rome are two shells corresponding
to Binah and Malkhut of holiness, and they are two clouds
(eyelids), right and left, that are male and female, and which
darken the light of Hokhmah that is drawn down from the
pupil of the eye. And these are the secret of the "wild beast of
the reeds" (Psalms 68:31), that was discussed above in the Zohar
(741), and they draw Hokhmah downwards from above, thus
covering the lights of Malkhut. And the cure for this is to
contract the upper three Sephirot of the left side, as is
explained there. And on the text: And what healing will there
be for them? This is the gall of a calf, for the gall is the secret
of the judgments of the Female that contract the upper three
Sephirot of the left side. (As above, 413, q.v.)

746) And for this reason, the chet, which is a thin thread
breaks and is replaced with a hey, turns the chamets [chet mem
tsade] into matsah [mem tsade hey] (as above, 741). For
initially, "The reeds and flags [suph] shall wither" (Isaiah 19:6).
'Reed' refers to the rule of Rome, which is an end [soph] for
all the kings, and which in the future of the Holy One, blessed
be He, will break. "Rebuke the wild beast of the reeds" (Psalms
68:31) means rebuke the wicked beast, which is the chet of

chamets [chet mem tsade], and the foot of the chet of machmetset is broken, as it is said: "Her feet go down to death" (Proverbs 5:5). Moreover: "Rebuke the wild beast of the reeds" (Psalms 68:31) means that He will break off the foot of the qoph of qaneh [qoph nun hey], and hineh [hey nun hey, behold] remains. Immediately: "Behold, the Lord God will come as a Mighty One, and His arm will rule for Him; Behold His reward is with Him and His recompense before Him" (Isaiah 40:10) and: "A harbinger unto Zion will I give: Behold, behold them; and to Jerusalem a messenger of good tidings" (Isaiah 41:27). The numerical value of 'behold' [hineh: hey nun hey, 5 + 50 + 5] is 60; i.e. sixty years after the year 5200 A.M., the verses quoted above will be fulfilled, as is clarified below. (These matters are explained above, 742, and below, 749.)

FOUR REDEMPTIONS

747) And the Holy Luminary said: "And all the souls belonging to Jacob... were sixty-six" (Genesis 46:26). Sixty is for the awakening of the first Messiah, and six is for the awakening of the second Messiah, and this leaves six years to go until the number 72, which is when the Redemption will take place, i.e. one thousand years, which is the whole of the fifth thousand that is destruction throughout, and 272 years into the sixth thousand (as above, 701), to establish therein the verse: "Six years shall you sow your field, and six years shall you prune your vineyard, and gather in the produce thereof" (Leviticus 25:3); i.e. twice six after one thousand and sixty years is the time for gathering in the produce thereof, i.e. the in gathering of the exiles, for Israel is called produce, as it is said: "Israel is the Lord's hallowed portion, the first-fruits of the produce" (Jeremiah 2:3).

748) This poses a question: If the Redemption is to be in the year 1272 A.M., what is the intent of the verse: "Sing [Ranu: resh nun waw, 200 + 50 + 6 = 256] with gladness for Jacob" (Jeremiah 31:7), which would seem to imply that the Redemption will be in the year 1256 A.M.? The answer to this is that there are to be four redemptions corresponding to the four cups of wine at the Passover Seder service, and they are the secret of Hokhmah and Binah, Tipheret and Malkhut, since Israel is scattered into the four directions of the world, which are the secret of Hokhmah and Binah, Tipheret and Malkhut, and those (of Israel) who are amongst the nations that are a long way away (from the Land of Israel), will be redeemed early, in the year 1256 A.M. The next group will be redeemed in the year 1260 A.M.; the third group in the year 1266 A.M.; and the fourth group in the year 1272 A.M.

749) And these redemptions will be with the four celestial beings of the Chariot: lion, ox, eagle, and man, in the name of the Tetragrammaton that rides on them, as it is written: "For You ride upon your horses, upon Your chariots of victory" (Habakkuk 3:8). Opposite them will awaken below four flags and twelve tribes, in the secret of the three Tetragrammatons: "The Tetragrammaton was king; the Tetragrammaton is king; the Tetragrammaton will be king forever and ever." As each Tetragrammaton has four letters, there are here twelve letters, corresponding to the twelve tribes, and the twelve faces of the three patriarchs, i.e. the three columns of Hesed, Gevurah, and Tipheret, about whom it has been said: The patriarchs are the Chariot (Midrash Bereshit Rabba, 47, 6), for the four heavenly beings are in the Chariot — the face of lion, ox, eagle, and man — and each has the three columns Hesed, Gevurah, and Tipheret, making twelve faces. And these ten tribes allude to a thousand years, while the other two tribes allude to two hundred years, and from the 12 letters of the three

Tetragrammatons are suspended the 72 Names, for these 12 letters are to be found in each Sephirah of Hesed, Gevurah, Tipheret, Netsach, Hod, and Yesod, of Ze'ir Anpin, and twelve (letters) multiplied by six (Sephirot) are 72. And these 72 are the years after one thousand and two hundred years (from the end of the fifth thousand since the creation of the world according to the traditional calculation). And from this is the allusion that the Redemption will come in the year 6272 A.M., as above. And it should be understood that all the apocalyptic dates mentioned in the Zohar imply that that is a favorable time for Israel to repent, and that their redemption is dependent on their repentance.

750) And they, the 72 Names, allot 24 to each of the celestial beings Hesed, Gevurah, Tipheret, which is to say as follows: If one divides the 72 Names between the six Sephirot Hesed, Gevurah, Tipheret, Netsach, Hod and Yesod, there will be 12 in each Sephirah, as above; but if one divides the 72 between the three Sephirot Hesed, Gevurah and Tipheret only, there will be 24 in each Sephirah, for 3 x 24 = 72. And the secret of 24 is: "And one called to the other and said: "Holy, holy, holy is the Lord of hosts" (Isaiah 6:3), they being three groups of angels, each consisting of 24 forms, where the first group says Holy, and the second group says Holy, and the third group says Holy. And all of this is in the illumination of the 72-letter Name, for the three groups together come to 72. The left immediately awakens with 42 letters, i.e. the 42-letter Name, that executes judgement on Amalek.

BIRD'S NEST

751) "If a bird's nest chance to be before you in the way, in any tree or on the ground, with young ones or eggs, and the

mother sitting upon the young, or upon the eggs, you shall not take the mother with the young" (Deuteronomy 22:6). "In the way" refers to the sages of the Bible, "in any tree" to the sages of the Mishnah, who are as young birds nestling in the branches of the tree. And there are those who say that "in any tree" refers to Israel about whom it is said: "For as the days of a tree shall be the days of My people" (Isaiah 65:22); and that "on the ground" refers to the sages of the Torah, about whom it is said: "Sleep on the ground and live a life of trouble while you toil in the Torah" (Mishnah, Pirkey Avot 6, 4). "Young ones" refers to young priests, and "eggs" are those whom the Holy One, blessed be He, nourishes — from buffalo's horns to louse's eggs (cf. Talmud Bavli, Shabbat 107b) — that is to say, including everything, from the smallest to the largest. "And the mother sitting upon the young" is the time when sacrifices used to be offered. What is written then? "You shall not take the mother with the young." That is to say: Do not break up the union of the mother, who is the Shekhinah, with the young, who are Israel.

752) After the destruction of the Temple and the annulment of the sacrifices, what is written? "You shall surely let the mother go, but the young you may take for yourself" (Deuteronomy 22:7), where the mother is the Shekhinah, and the young have been exiled. For the Kabbalists are called 'young' or 'sons,' for they are from the side of the letter aleph that is inserted in the spelling of the letter waw filled out, i.e. waw aleph waw of the Tetragrammaton [yod hey waw and hey], which is a long world, for this letter aleph that is inserted in the filled out waw [waw aleph waw], is drawn down from Binah, which is the secret of the world to come, which is a world that is altogether long, about which it is said: "So that it may be well with you and that you may prolong your days" (Deuteronomy 22:7) in the world that is altogether long (cf. Talmud Bavli, Kiddushin 39b).

753) And in the Exile, prayer was decreed instead of sacrifices, and Israel chirped away with the sound of the songs of the recital of the Shema Israel, which ascends to the central column that is on high, i.e. Ze'ir Anpin, for the mother and the daughter, which are Binah and Malkhut, are in exile, for inasmuch as Malkhut is composed of Binah, to that extent Binah is also in exile, and immediately on Ze'ir Anpin's descent, He is joined with the daughter, which is Malkhut, that is called weak hand, in order to connect the waw, which is Ze'ir Anpin, with the hey, which is Malkhut in six Sephirot, for the recital of the Shema Israel is the drawing down of the six intermediate Sephirot of Gadlut to Ze'ir Anpin and Malkhut. Immediately, "Blessed be the name of the glory of His kingdom forever and ever" [insertion after the first line of the recital of the Shema Israel] is whispered to Hokhmah [it being said silently — tr.], for it is the secret of the unity of Malkhut, to which the emanation is then drawn down from Hokhmah.

THE FOUR SECTIONS IN THE PHYLACTERIES AND OF THE RECITAL OF THE SHEMA ISRAEL

754) The numerical value of 'one' [echad: aleph chet dalet, 1 + 8 + 4 = 13], the final word of the first line of the Shema Israel, together with the numerical value of 'glory' [kavod: kaph beit waw dalet, 20 + 2 + 6 + 4 = 32], from the inserted silent response after the first line of the Shema Israel, add up to 45, which is the mem hey (40 + 5 = 45) from Hokhmah [chet kaph mem hey]. For Hokhmah is brought down to Mother, and immediately on the descent of Hokhmah to Mother, the people bind it with the knot of the head phylactery, for the knot of the head phylactery is the secret of Leah, which is the secret of dry land (as above, in the Introduction to the Sepher ha-Zohar, 205-206), who is the one to receive from descending Hokhmah,

in the secret of the verse: "And you shall see My back" (Exodus 33:23), that turns on the knot of the head phylactery. And for this reason, the four sections of the phylacteries are: 1) "Sanctify unto Me" (Exodus 13:1-10), which is Hokhmah; 2) "And it shall be when the Lord shall bring you into the land" (Exodus 13:11-16), which is Binah; 3) "Hear, O Israel" (Deuteronomy 6:4-9), which is Tipheret, consisting of six Sephirot in the six words of the Shema Israel: Hear, O-Israel, the-Lord, our-God, the-Lord is-one; 4) "And it shall come to pass, if you shall hearken diligently unto My commandments which I command you this day" (Deuteronomy 11:13-21), which is Malkhut that is called weak hand. The prayer is Keter (crown), i.e. a crown on the head of Ze'ir Anpin, in the secret of the verse: "There is none holy as the Lord" (I Samuel 2:2), where the letter kaph (meaning 'as') alludes to Keter [kaph tav resh] (as above, 572), because (the angel) Sandalphon ties all the prayers together and makes them into a crown (cf. Talmud Bavli, Hagigah 13b, and see Tosaphot there).

755) At that time the table has to be prepared for the king's banquet, and the tabernacle and candelabra and the ark and the altar and all sorts of utensils of the king's house have to be arranged. And we do not refer to just any table that is not made by the Holy One, blessed be He, for we are referring to none other than the table which is made by the Holy One, blessed be He, which is His Shekhinah. And the Shekhinah is Ze'ir Anpin's tabernacle, His table, His candelabra, His ark, His altar, for it, the Shekhinah, is made up of all the utensils of the upper king, who is Ze'ir Anpin.

THE SHEW-BREAD THAT HAS 12 COUNTENANCES

756) Those who are called sons are the ones who arrange the

wine and bread of the upper king, Ze'ir Anpin, and about
them it is said: "My food which is presented to Me for
offerings made by fire" (Numbers 28:2). For only those that are
called the fire-offerings of the Lord may be offered to Him (as
was explained above, 509, q.v.), and it is therefore written: "My
food which is presented to Me for offerings made by fire"
(ibid.). For it is said about it: "Come, eat of my bread"
(Proverbs 9:5), and they are called the shew-bread (literally: the
bread of the countenances), there being 12 countenances that
are alluded to in the three Tetragrammatons (of the priestly
benediction): "The Tetragrammaton bless you... The
Tetragrammaton make His face to shine... The Tetragrammaton
lift up His countenance..." (Numbers 6:24-26). Each
Tetragrammaton has four letters, and there are thus 12 that
correspond to the 12 countenances of three celestial beings.

COMMENTARY:

Although the celestial beings are four in numbers — lion, ox,
eagle, man — when they are included within each other, each
celestial being does not include all four beings, but three beings
— lion, ox, and eagle — making 12 countenances, while man is
missing from each of the four celestial beings; and even in man
himself there are only lion, ox, and eagle, while the face of
man, which is the aspect of himself, is not there. And the
reason is that the face of man is really Malkhut in the aspect
of itself, which is the secret of the Lock, which they do not
have, for they have only Malkhut of the Key, which is
mitigated with Binah, which is the aspect of the diadem of
Yesod of Ze'ir Anpin, and not Malkhut in actuality (as above,
in the Introduction of the Sepher ha-Zohar, pages 45 and 47).

And it is therefore included within eagle, which is Ze'ir Anpin, and the real face of a man, which is Malkhut in the aspect of itself, is non-existent there. (See above, Bereshit Beit, page 158.)

757) What is the bread of these 12 countenances? It is the bread of man, which is the secret of the Tetragrammaton, filled in with alephs, thus yod = yod waw dalet, 10 + 6 + 4 = 20; hey = hey aleph, 5 + 1 = 6; waw = waw aleph waw, 6 + 1 + 6 = 13; hey = hey aleph, 5 + 1 = 6; and 20 + 6 + 13 + 6 = 45, which is the numerical equivalent of man [adam: aleph dalet mem, 1 + 4 + 40 = 45]. And they are 12 in the secret of the three Tetragrammatons, which means the three columns, in each of which is one Tetragrammaton, making a total of 12 letters, as above. And He has bread in four faces, which are the four letters of the Tetragrammaton [yod hey waw and hey], that include 12 faces, as above. This bread of the king's table is clean fine flour, that contains no chaff or straw, which are judgments.

COMMENTARY:

The bread is the 12 countenances of Ze'ir Anpin, and it is arranged on the table, which is Malkhut, that is called the king's table.

758) His oven, in which he bakes the bread, is the Shekhinah,

for the bread cooks and is completed there. And this is why one should not start cutting the bread other than at the point where its cooking was completed, i.e. it is similar to the perfection of a piece of fruit that has reached full ripeness. And this is 'The Lord' [aleph dalet nun yod], which is Malkhut, which is completion and perfection of the Tetragrammaton [yod hey waw and hey], which is Ze'ir Anpin, which is the shew-bread, i.e. the twelve countenances mentioned above which are in Ze'ir Anpin. 'The Lord' [aleph dalet nun yod] is Ze'ir Anpin's oven and completes Him. And it is called an oven [kivshan: kaph beit shin nun] because it is subdued [kevushah: kaph beit waw shin hey] under its husband, and for her it is it said: "Now Mount Sinai was altogether on smoke, because the Lord descended upon it in fire; and the smoke thereof ascended as the smoke of a furnace" (Exodus 19:18). "Furnace" [kivshan] here does not mean an ordinary furnace, but rather that in which He applies [kovesh] His mercies to His people when they pray and present their supplications. And so is it said: May Your mercy suppress [yikhbeshu] Your anger (Talmud Bavli, Berakhot 7a). And in the same context: What do you have to do with the secrets [kaph beit shin] of the Merciful One? (cf. Talmud Balvi, Berakhot 10a, bot.), for the secrets of the Holy One, blessed be He, are called kivshe (secrets) of the Merciful One.

759) And in the bread of the Torah there is clean pure flour, which the King gives to those about whom it is said: All Israel are the sons of kings (cf. Talmud Bavli, Shabbat 128a), i.e. He gives it to those who are called sons, for it is the food of the righteous. And there is also bread of the Torah that is waste matter and which is given to the servants and bondwomen of the king's house, who attend to the horses and riders of the king's house (as below, 762), and for this reason it is said about the queen: "She rises also while it is yet night, and gives food

to her household, and a portion to her maidens" (Proverbs
31:15), who are the sages of the Mishnah. And this is why it is
said about the food of the king: "And the tenth part of an
ephah of fine flour" (Numbers 28:5). Fine flour, certainly;
while the tenth part of an ephah is the yod (whose numerical
value is ten) of 'The Lord' [aleph dalet nun yod], which is
certainly the tenth, and it follows that this fine flour is the
food of the king, as above.

760) The Faithful Shepherd said: Rise up, Holy Luminary, you
and Rabbi Elazar, your son, together with Rabbi Abba, Rabbi
Yehudah, Rabbi Yossi, Rabbi Hiyya and Rabbi Yudai, to
prepare a gift for the King, the Holy One, blessed be He, to
make a sacrifice of all the limbs, which are Israel, so that they
should be sacrificial offerings to the Holy One, blessed be He.
And those who are called the souls [neshamah] of Israel are
offered to the limbs of the holy Shekhinah, i.e. to the Sephirot
of Malkhut, which is called fire of the Most High, and this fire
is attached to the pieces of wood [ets] that are called "the wood
[ets] of the burnt-offering" (Genesis 22:6), namely, the Tree
[ets] of Life, which is Ze'ir Anpin, and the Tree [ets] of the
Knowledge of Good and Evil (see Genesis 2:17), which is
Malkhut. Trees of holiness is the name given to the sages of
Torah, for the Torah is attached to them, as it is said: "Is not
My word like as fire, says the Lord" (Jeremiah 23:29).

MY FOOD WHICH IS PRESENTED TO ME FOR
OFFERINGS MADE BY FIRE

761) It is said about Malkhut: "A burnt-offering unto the
Lord" (Numbers 28:11), "an offering unto the Lord" (Leviticus
27:9), "an offering made by fire unto the Lord" (Numbers 28:6),
and it is said: "My food which is presented to Me for offerings

made by fire" (ibid. v.2). And has it not already been written:
Sacrifices must be offered to none other than God? (cf. Talmud
Bavli, Menachot 110a bot. on Psalms 1:11). What, therefore, is
the meaning of "offering made by fire" (Numbers 28:2)?
[Understood as: offerings made to fire — which is a possible
translation — tr.]. The answer here is that one who offers a gift
does so for the king, and the king distributes it to whomsoever
he pleases. Israel, likewise, offers the Torah, which is Malkhut,
to the Holy One, blessed be He, that is His bread and His wine
and His meat. And it is said about it, about the Torah, which is
Malkhut, "bone of my bones and flesh of my flesh" (Genesis
2:23). And this is holy flesh, about which the teachers of the
academy taught: We are talking about flesh that descends from
heaven (cf. Talmud Bavli, Sanhedrin 59b).

COMMENTARY:

By means of the sacrifice that Israel offers, the souls
[neshamah] are offered to Malkhut, in the secret of Female
Waters, and Malkhut is itself offered to the King, i.e. the unity
is effected of Ze'ir Anpin and Malkhut, and the King
distributes to all the worlds from the illumination of this
mating.

FINE FLOUR, MEDIUM FLOUR AND WASTE MATTER

762) What does the Holy One, blessed be He, do with this gift,
i.e. with the illumination of the mating made by the sacrifice,
as above? He is like a king who eats at his own table, and
every type is served at the table: fine flour, medium flour, and

waste matter, and he distributes from his table to all those
sitting at the banquet, through his appointees, to each one as
befits him. He commands that bread made out of fine flour
that the King eats be given to those he loves who are near to
him as it is written: "My food which is presented to Me for
offerings made by fire, of a sweet savor" (Numbers 28:2), i.e.:
"They shall eat the offerings of the Lord made by fire and His
inheritance" (Deuteronomy 18:1). And this food is from the side
of the Tree of Life and is, therefore, clean fine flour, without
any waste matter at all. But from the side of the Tree of
Knowledge of Good and Evil, in which there is waste matter,
which is the medium flour, He commanded to be given to the
angels, while the waste matter He gives to the shades and
demons who serve as the horses and riders of the king.

763) And here, too, the medium flour is given to the king's
horsemen, namely the sages of Mishnah, who are as the angels,
and their batmen are the Jewish shades [shade in Hebrew is
shed: shin dalet], for they are written with the first two letters
[shin dalet] of Shadday [Almighty, shin dalet yod]. And there
are also shades and demons from the side of impurity that are
called idol-worshipping shades, for "God made the one to
correspond with the other" (Ecclesiastes 7:14).

764) And for this reason the sages of the Mishnah said: There
are three things about the demons of Jews: in one respect they
are like the ministering angels; in a second respect they are like
human beings; and, in a third respect they are like animals, and
some of them are scholars in the Written Law and the Oral
Law. (Cf. Talmud Bavli, Hagigah 16a: Six things have been said
about shades...) And he who is called Joseph the Shade is so
called because he sired a shade. And it was not for nothing that
the sages of the Mishnah said: If the rabbi is similar to an
angel of the Lord of Hosts, let them seek Torah from his

mouth (Talmud Bavli, Hagigah 15b). For the sages of the Mishnah are likened to the angels (as above, 763). And Ashmadai, king of the shades, and all his family are, it has been taught, Jewish shades, for they have submitted to the Torah and the names of the Torah.

765) And because the sons of Aaron arranged their sacrifices, this is why they were punished, for even though all the sacrifices are offered to the king, the king distributes them to each one, as befits him, and takes for himself what befits him.

COMMENTARY:

The emanation of the sacrifice is subdivided into three parts: a) Clean pure flour, which is the secret of the emanation of hasadim that are drawn down from Ze'ir Anpin, for the shell has no hold in hasadim, which is why it is called pure flour, alluding to the fact that there is no waste matter in it.

b) Medium flour, which is the illumination of the six intermediate Sephirot of Hokhmah that is drawn down from Malkhut, which is the secret of the illumination of Hokhmah, upwards from below.

c) Waste matter, i.e. the illumination of Hokhmah that is drawn downwards from above, for this was the sin of the Tree of Knowledge of Good and Evil (see Genesis 2).

And on the text (762): "And he distributes from his table to all those sitting at the banquet." For Israel offers the sacrifice of the mating of Ze'ir Anpin and Malkhut, from the illumination

of which mating issues forth three types of emanation, which
Ze'ir Anpin Himself distributes. And "that bread is made out
of fine flour that the king eats." For Ze'ir Anpin is in the
secret of: "Because he delights in loving kindness hesed"
(Michah 7:18), and he therefore eats the fine flour, which is
the secret of the light of hasadim. He commands that it be
given to those he loves, for it is the food of the lovers who
cleave to hesed as does Ze'ir Anpin. And on the text: "Is from
the side of the Tree of Life;" i.e. from the side of Ze'ir Anpin,
who is called the Tree of Life, from which the emanation of
hasadim is drawn down. "But from the side of the Tree of
Knowledge of Good and Evil," which is Malkhut, from which
the emanation of Hokhmah is drawn down. "Which is the
medium flour... given to the angels." i.e. medium flour which is
the secret of the six intermediate Sephirot of Hokhmah, i.e.
which illuminates upwards from below.

And on the text (763): "And here, too, the medium flour is
given to the king's horsemen, namely, the sages of the
Mishnah." And indeed the sages of the Mishnah, who cleave to
Malkhut, that is called Mishnah, also receive medium flour. But
(762) the waste matter he gives to the shades and demons, for
the waste matter is the secret of the drawing down of
Hokhmah, downwards from above, which illumination is
forbidden and is comparable to impure blood, as above (379, in
the Commentator's Interpolation, par. 12, q.v.), and is given to
the shadem and demons. Although this illumination is also
drawn by Israel when they offer sacrifices, it is not considered
a sin for them, for this illumination issues of necessity (as
above, Bereshit Aleph, page 80), and it is not they who draw it
down and distribute it to the side of impurity, namely the
shadem and demons, but Ze'ir Anpin who thus distributes the
emanation. However, the sons of Aaron arranged all three of
these drawing downs by themselves, even including the

third, forbidden, drawing down, and gave it to the shadem and demons.

And on the text (765): "And because the sons of Aaron arranged their sacrifices." Because they themselves drew down and arranged all three of the above-mentioned drawing downs and distributed them. "This is why they were punished." They were punished because the third drawing down that they drew down from above is forbidden to Israel, as above. And this is despite the fact that in all the sacrifices these illuminations go forth to the shadem and demons, for it is then by the instrumentally of Ze'ir Anpin, from above, for He distributes them according to His will. And on the text: "For even though all the sacrifices are offered to the king;" then all three types of illumination — fine flour, medium flour, and waste matter — issue forth, and there is here no prohibition because "the king distributes them to each one, as befits him, and takes for himself what befits him." For Ze'ir Anpin distributes and arranges the three types of emanation and gives the third type to the shadem and demons, as he wishes. But Israel, who are the ones to offer the sacrifices, have no part of this, which was not the case with the sons of Aaron who themselves arranged three types of emanation, and they themselves distributed it. They were therefore punished, because of the drawing down of the third type.

THE FEAST OF WEEKS

766) "Also in the day of the first-fruits, when you bring a new meal offering to the Lord in your feast of weeks" (Numbers 28:26). Rabbi Abba said: It is written "the day of the first-fruits," but who does "day" refer to? The answer is that this is a river issuing forth from Eden, i.e. Ze'ir Anpin, who is

a day of those upper first-fruits, namely yod hey, Father and
Mother, who are called first-fruits. And this is the one upon
whom the Torah depends, i.e. Ze'ir Anpin, and he brings forth
all the secrets of the Torah, and because he is the Tree of Life,
the fruit of the tree has to be brought.

THE FAITHFUL SHEPHERD

767) "Also in the day of the first-fruits, when you bring a
new meal offering to the Lord in your feast of weeks"
(Numbers 28:26). Rabbi Abba said: "The day of the first-fruits"
refers to the upper first-fruits of the Torah, namely, Father
and Mother, as it is written: "The choicest first-fruits of your
land you shall bring into the house of the Lord your God"
(Exodus 23:19). Said the Faithful Shepherd: Just as the
first-born to their mother are called bikkurim, so are the
first-fruits of the tree called bikkurim: "I found Israel like
grapes in the wilderness; I saw your fathers as the first-ripe
and the fig-tree at her season" (Hosea 9:10). So, too, is Israel
the first-ripe and the first-fruits for the Holy One, blessed be
He, of all the nations of the world, as it is written: "Israel is
the Lord's hallowed portion, His first-fruits of the increase"
(Jeremiah 2:3). For this reason it is said about them, about the
first-fruits that allude to Israel: "The choicest first-fruits of
your land you shall bring into the house of the Lord your God"
(Exodus 23:19), i.e. that they should merit complete
redemption. And for this reason it is said about the idolatrous
nation: "All that devour him shall be held guilty; evil shall
come upon them" (Jeremiah 2:3); and also: "And they devour
Israel with open mouth" (Isaiah 9:12).

768) And so, too, waw, which is Ze'ir Anpin, that includes six
Sephirot, and which is Ben Yah, which are Father and Mother

that are called bikkurim [first-fruits; root: beit kaph resh], is called beit kaph resh. And all the branches that come out from it and in which there are heads, the levels which contain the upper three Sephirot that are termed head, are called bikkurim (first-fruits). Waw is a river of those upper first-fruits, which is Ze'ir Anpin, and this is the river that comes out of Eden (see Genesis 2:10), which is Yah [yod hey], and it is on this that the Torah is dependent. Then all secrets of the Torah are revealed. And because it is both the Tree of Life and the Torah, it is written: "It is a tree of life to those that lay hold upon it" (Proverbs 3:18). And the precepts of Ze'ir Anpin, who is the Torah, are like the buds of the fruit of the tree that have to be brought to the house of the Lord.

769) Said the Faithful Shepherd: You might wish to ask: Why are the first-fruits, that are called "a new meal offering" (Numbers 28:26), to be found on the tree from six months to six months? That is, during the six months of the winter and autumn they are on the tree as a foetus in its mother's womb, and from when they start growing until they are fully ripe another six months pass. What is the reason for this taking six months? And again, about man it is said: "For man is as the tree of the field" (Deuteronomy 20:19). What is the reason for his having a nine or seven-month gestation period? And it is also said about cattle: "It shall be seven days under the dam, but from the eighth day and onwards it may be accepted for an offering made by fire to the Lord" (Leviticus 22:27), i.e. to be offered as a sacrifice before the Lord. And what is the reason for the seven days being required? Futhermore, why are the Sephirot, in which are the name of the Tetragrammaton [yod hey waw and hey] and all His other Names, called by the names of the celestial beings, i.e. lion, ox, eagle, and man?

770) The answer is that "a new meal offering" (Numbers 28:26) is to be understood by way of secret, and its meaning is the

Shekhinah. From six months to six months that the fruits are
gestating on the tree refers to the six Sephirot — Hesed,
Gevurah, Tipheret, Netsach, Hod, and Yesod which are called
the primordial years of the creation of the world, which are the
secret of the six thousand years that the world has been in
existence, and they are called years from the point of view of
upper Mother, which is Binah, while from the point of view of
lower Mother, which is Malkhut, they are called months. And
because these six Sephirot preceded the world and all the
creatures, they are called first-fruits, and this is the secret of
the six months of the fruit of the tree, which are the
first-fruits, from the time they start growing until they are
fully ripe, i.e. corresponding to Hesed, Gevurah, Tipheret,
Netsach, Hod, and Yesod from the point of view of Malkhut.

771) And the Shekhinah, which is "a new meal offering"
(Numbers 28:26) is, from the point of view of the celestial
being, about whom it is said "And the likeness of their faces as
the face of a man" (Ezekiel 1:10), the nine months of gestation,
for the numerical value of 'man' [adam: aleph dalet mem, 1 + 4
+ 4 = 9] is nine in the small calculation of Enokh, for in the
secret of the small number, which is Metatron, who is called
Enokh, the value of the letters is considered only as a number
of units, such that the letter mem (usual numerical value = 40)
will be only 4, and so, too, tav (usual numerical value = 400)
will be only 4, and so on, so that the numerical value of man
[adam: aleph dalet mem] works out to (1 + 4 + 4) just nine.
And this is the secret of man, who is born after nine months of
gestation. And man who is born is the tenth for them and is
thereby included in all ten of the Sephirot. And man is called
the first-born son, after the name of the sign of the covenant,
which is Yesod, which is yod, named after the first drop drawn
out of him, seed shot straight as an arrow, from which man is
born, and every drop is called yod (whose numerical value

is ten), because it includes ten Sephirot. And it, Yesod, is waw (numerical value of 6) and is the drop, being yod that rises over waw, which is Yesod, just as the fruit rises over the branch of the tree. And because there are three upper Sephirot, which is the secret of bikkurim, first-fruits, in the ten Sephirot, man is therefore called ben bekhor, the first-born son.

772) And although there are a number of branches on the tree, on which are a number of figs, those that ripen first at the beginning are called bikkurim, the first-fruits. And these are the heads of all of them, and on a parallel with them it is said: "Lift up your heads, O gates" (Psalms 24:7), the meaning of which is: "Lift up your eyes on high and see: Who has created these?" (Isaiah 40:26); and also: "Take the sum of all the congregation of the children of Israel" [literally: Lift up the head of all the congregation of the children of Israel] (Numbers 1:2).

COMMENTARY:

He says that the reason why man is called a first-born son is that he comes from a drop of Yesod, which is the secret of yod (whose numerical value is ten), which is composed of ten Sephirot. Amongst these ten are the three upper Sephirot Keter, Hokhmah and Binah, which are called bikkurim, first-fruits. According to this, all mortals should be called bekhorim, first-born, but only the first son is so called. And so that you should not find this difficult to understand, he says (772): "And although there are a number of branches on the tree, on which are a number of figs, those that ripen first at the beginning are called bikkurim, the first-fruits." For the revelation of the upper three Sephirot, that are called bikkurim, is only on the first-fruit and on the first son, and the upper three Sephirot are not revealed on the remaining sons, even though they are drawn down from the yod. And on the text: "And these are the heads of all of them." For the first son is the head, or chief, over all those that come after him, that is to say, the upper three Sephirot that are called head are revealed on him, and from him the head illuminates to the other sons. And the proof that head means the upper three Sephirot is taken from the Scriptural verse: "Lift up your head, O gates" (Psalms 24:70), where the word for "Lift up" means the upper three Sephirot, as in the verse: "Lift up your eyes on high and see: Who has created these?" (Isaiah 40:26), where its meaning is the upper three Sephirot because "your eyes" is the secret of Hokhmah. And also: "Take the sum of all of the congregation of the children of Israel" [literally: Lift up the head of all the congregation of the children of Israel] (Numbers 1:2) refers to the upper three Sephirot. Thus the bikkurim, first-fruits, are called heads, after the upper three Sephirot.

773) "Lift up your heads, O gates" (Psalms 24:7). Gates here are the fifty gates of Binah which are the Heavenly Academy. "And be lifted up, O everlasting doors" (ibid.) refers to the doors of the Earthly Academy, which is Malkhut, for everyone who engages in the Torah is, at the end, exalted, as it is written: "If you have acted foolishly in lifting yourself up" (Proverbs 30:32). And the sages of the Mishnah taught: Whoever abases himself (acts foolishly) for words of the Torah will, in the end, be exalted (cf. Talmud Bavli, Berakhot 63b).

And this is the meaning of "That the King of glory may come

in" (Psalms 24:7), for there is no glory apart from the Torah (Mishnah, Pirkey Avot, 6, 3).

774) It follows that whoever learns Torah, which is called glory, is himself called a king (cf. Talmud Bavli, Gittin 62a), for it is written "That the King of glory may come in" (Psalms 24:7). And it should not be said that he is a king in the next world and no more than that, for he is a king in both the worlds, in the form of his Master. And this is why the verse comes twice: "Who is the King of glory?" (ibid. v.7) and "Who then is the King of glory?" (ibid. v.10), which teaches that the reference is to both the worlds, this world and the world to come. The verse "Lift up your heads, O gates" (ibid. verses 7 and 9) appears twice. What is the meaning of 'your heads?' The answer to this is that on the one occasion they refer to the celestial beings of the heavenly chariot, which is above the chest of Ze'ir Anpin; and on the other occasion they refer to the celestial beings of the lower chariot that are in Malkhut.

775) Rabbi Shimeon unravelled a verse, saying: "Lift up your heads, O gates" (Psalms 24:7). This verse has been taught and we have learned it. "Lift up your heads, O gates," these are the upper gates, the gates of upper understanding, and they are fifty in number. "Your heads." What heads does this refer to? The answer is that each one, i.e. each gate, has a head to be enclothed and enter in to one another and to be incorporated within each other.

776) I found in the Book of Enokh: "Lift up, O gates" (Psalms 24:7). These are the gates that are below the Patriarchs, i.e. below Hesed, Gevurah, and Tipheret, which are called patriarchs, and they are the three last Sephirot, namely Netsach, Hod, and Yesod. "Your heads" (ibid.) are the heads of the thousand of Israel, and they are the upper patriarchs,

namely Hesed, Gevurah, and Tipheret, which, at the time of fullness, become Hokhmah, Binah, and Da'at, and they are the heads of those gates. And for the sake of these — Netsach, Hod, and Yesod — which are the Ophanim that encompass and bear them on their shoulders, it is said: "Lift up your heads, O gates" (ibid.). Lift up whom? Your heads, for they, Hesed, Gevurah, and Tipheret, are heads, chiefs, over you and have control over you. "And be lifted up, O everlasting doors" (ibid.): These are the Matriarchs, and they are four who are below, namely Hesed, Gevurah, Tipheret, and Malkhut, that are in Malkhut, where Sarah is Hesed, Rebecca is Gevurah, Leah is Tipheret, and Rachel is Malkhut.

COMMENTARY:

From the chest and upwards of Ze'ir Anpin is the secret of Hesed, Gevurah and Tipheret, and they are with hasadim covered with Hokhmah; while from the chest and below of Ze'ir Anpin is the place where Hokhmah is revealed, but hasadim are lacking. And Hokhmah is unable to illuminate without hasadim, and for Ze'ir Anpin to mate with Malkhut it is first necessary that Netsach, Hod, and Yesod, and Hesed, Gevurah, and Tipheret be comprised of each other; and then Netsach, Hod, and Yesod have Hokhmah and hasadim together, and they are able to illuminate and can then emanate to Malkhut. Likewise, Hesed, Gevurah, and Tipheret, which are hasadim, are perfected by the revelation of Hokhmah that is in Netsach, Hod, and Yesod. And it is then discernible that Netsach, Hod, and Yesod are gates to Hesed, Gevurah, and Tipheret, for it is impossible to receive the perfect illumination of hasadim from Hesed, Gevurah, and Tipheret of Ze'ir Anpin before Hokhmah is revealed in Netsach, Hod, and Yesod of

Ze'ir Anpin, since, without them, the hasadim that are in
Hesed, Gevurah, and Tipheret are comparable to the aspect of
the six intermediate Sephirot without a head. But after the
revelation of Hokhmah in Netsach, Hod, and Yesod, Hesed,
Gevurah, and Tipheret, and Netsach, Hod and Yesod are
composed of each other, and Hesed, Gevurah, and Tipheret are
comparable to heads, for they have thereby come into the
aspect of the upper three Sephirot that are called heads in such
a way that Netsach, Hod, and Yesod are gates through which
Hesed, Gevurah, and Tipheret are raised to the aspect of heads.
And on the text: "And for the sake of these... which are the
Ophanim that encompass and bear them on their shoulders."
For Netsach, Hod, and Yesod of Ze'ir Anpin are called
Ophanim, and they bear Hesed, Gevurah, and Tipheret of Ze'ir
Anpin on their shoulders, that is to say that they are the ones
that lift them up to the aspect of heads. And the use of the
expression 'on their shoulders' alludes to the fact that, like the
shoulders of a man that support his head, so do Netsach, Hod,
and Yesod hold Hesed, Gevurah, and Tipheret up to the aspect
of head. And on the text: ...is it said: "Lift up your heads, O
gates" (Psalms 24:7). Lift up whom? "Your heads, for they... are
heads, chiefs, over you and have control over you." Which is
why we say to Netsach, Hod, and Yesod: Lift up your heads, O
gates, that they should lift Hesed, Gevurah, and Tipheret up to
be heads. 'Over you' means the same as 'for your sakes.' And
on the text: For they... are... over you and have control over
you," because for your sakes they are heads and rulers, i.e. the
upper three Sephirot, which are termed head and ruler, are
revealed through your instrumentality: "And be lifted up, O
everlasting doors" (ibid.): i.e. emanating and lifting up Malkhut
also.

777) "That the King of glory may come" (Psalms 24:7) This is
the supreme King over all, i.e. Ze'ir Anpin, which includes
Hesed, Gevurah, and Tipheret and also Netsach, Hod, and
Yesod, for he is king of that same glory that gives light to the
moon, which is Malkhut, that is called glory. And who is this?
It is "The Lord of Hosts" (ibid. v.10), i.e. Ze'ir Anpin, who is
so called. It is written "That the King of glory may come" (ibid.
v.7), and the question is put: To what place will he come? And
the answer is, to bring the Torah, which is Ze'ir Anpin, in the
Ark, which is Malkhut, in one union as is fitting. For after the
former has entered his place, i.e. after Ze'ir Anpin has mated
with Malkhut which is his place, it is then discernible that the
Torah, which is an aspect of Ze'ir Anpin, has entered the Ark,
which is an aspect of Malkhut. And they have become joined
together in one union, the upper Torah which is an aspect of
Ze'ir Anpin with the Oral Torah, which is an aspect of
Malkhut, for they join together in order to interpret hidden
matters, i.e. to reveal the secrets of the Torah to the righteous.

778) The question is put: When is this unity made? And the
answer is given: About this it is written: "Also in the day of the
first-fruits, when you bring a new meal offering to the Lord in
your feast of weeks" (Numbers 28:26). And the meaning of "in
your weeks" is according to your reckoning, for whenever
Israel makes calculations regarding the new moons and
festivals, the Holy One, blessed be He, sets an Ark within the
heavens, i.e. one that is like the ark of the reader (at a
synagogue service), and issues a proclamation: My sons on earth
have sanctified the month (or) have sanctified the festival,
(therefore) sanctify yourselves, all of you in heaven, and He
sees to it that all the hosts of the heavens become sanctified as
one with the holy people and they all observe (the new moon
or the festival) at the same time, on the same day that Israel
determined on earth. Therefore it is written: "In your weeks"

(ibid.), i.e. according to your reckoning of these seven weeks (see Leviticus 23:15).

YOU SHALL SURELY LET THE DAM GO

779) And then the Holy One, blessed be He, draws down seven stages with that stage, i.e. with Malkhut, which unites with them, with those seven weeks, which are the secret of Hesed, Gevurah, and Tipheret and Netsach, Hod, Yesod, and Malkhut. And should you suggest that there are six stages, and no more, namely Hesed, Gevurah, and Tipheret and Netsach, Hod and Yesod, for Malkhut is the one that receives from them and is not part of the reckoning, the answer would be: Then Mother, i.e. Binah, is "sitting upon the young" (See Deuteronomy 22:6), which are Hesed, Gevurah, and Tipheret and Netsach, Hod, Yesod, and Malkhut, and is to be found brooding over them, hatching out Binah from them, and taking those six young ones, namely Hesed, Gevurah, and Tipheret and Netsach, Hod, and Yesod, with the stage that is below them, namely, Malkhut, to fulfill the scriptural verse: "You shall surely let the dam go, but the young you may take for yourself" (Deuteronomy 22:7), where the dam is Binah and the young are Hesed, Gevurah, and Tipheret and Netsach, Hod, Yesod, and Malkhut. And we therefore count seven weeks (from Passover to the Feast of Weeks), drawing down seven Sephirot, i.e. Malkhut also, and having drawn down Malkhut also, we draw down Hesed, Gevurah, and Tipheret and Netsach, Hod, and Yesod to include them in Malkhut.

ISRAEL KNOWS HOW TO HUNT WELL

780) Rav Hamnuna Saba said: On that day Israel takes only

five sons, which are the five books of the Pentateuch, i.e.
Hesed, Gevurah, Tipheret, Netsach and Hod of Ze'ir Anpin,
which are the five parts of Ze'ir Anpin, who is called Torah.
And should you object, saying that the Sephirot are six in
number, for there is also Yesod, the truth really is that there
are seven, together with a certain bird, which is Malkhut, and
they are to be found between the wings of Mother, which is
Binah. And the reason why he thought initially that there were
only five main stages, Hesed, Gevurah, Tipheret, Netsach,
Hod, with Yesod and Malkhut being composed of those five
stages, and containing nothing new. And Israel knows how to
hunt well for good and valuable game. What do they do? They
draw out that bird, which is Malkhut, from under the wings of
Mother with slight sounds from the mouth that they whisper to
her, one after the other, i.e. with many prayers.

781) And that bird becomes excited at those whispers and the
sounds that they voice to her under their breath, and, even
though she is under the wings of Mother, she raises her head
and looks out at the whispering voice and bursts out to them,
emerging from under the wings of Mother. So Israel takes her
and holds her, whispering to her and tying her with a knot so
that she will not fly off and leave. Israel immediately catches
her in this knot, and the bird wants to fly off and leave them
but is unable to do so.

782) And while she is still bound in the hands of Israel, they
whisper their sounds, and she chirps with them, and flies up
and down. And all those sons who are under the wings of their
Mother, namely, Hesed, Gevurah, and Tipheret and Netsach,
Hod, Yesod, of Ze'ir Anpin, when they hear the chirping of
their sister, Malkhut, and the sound of that whisper from
Israel, they immediately emerge from under the wings of their
Mother and fly towards that bird, which is Malkhut, and Israel

takes them and unites with them. And had it not been for that bird, with which they were attached initially, they — Hesed, Gevurah, Tipheret, Netsach, Hod, and Yesod — would never have flown to them (to Israel), and they would not have been able to unite with them.

783) How does one catch this holy bird? This is done by preparing before her valuable food with rejoicing, and all sorts of pleasantries, and attending the synagogue and the school-house, and chirping at her in a voice of whispers, as is fitting. And she, the bird, who is hiding under the wings of Mother, raises her head and looks at the prepared tables, with the chirping which is for her, i.e. the prayers, as is fitting, and she emerges from under the wings of Mother, and flies to them, as we have learned, and all those sons, namely Hesed, Gevurah, Tipheret, Netsach, Hod and Yesod of Ze'ir Anpin, take hold of her.

784) And they send the one who is sitting over them, i.e. Mother, which is Binah, which is sitting over Hesed, Gevurah, Tipheret, Netsach, Hod, Yesod, and Malkhut, and she goes off. Because from the seventh heaven, which is Hesed, and above, i.e. the upper three Sephirot, (we have learned:) Do not expound what is hidden from you (cf. Talmud Bavli, Hagigah 13a). Therefore, send her away, that is, the mother, which is Binah, which is one of the upper three Sephirot, for you will not be able to catch her. About this Scripture says: "You shall surely let the dam go, but the young you may take for yourself" (Deuteronomy 22:7), the meaning of which is that you should not try to persue Binah, for she is not within reach. But the young, namely Hesed, Gevurah, Tipheret, Netsach, Hod, Yesod, and Malkhut, which are within reach, you may take for yourself.

785) "You shall have a holy convocation [miqra,' from the root qoph resh aleph]" (Numbers 28:26). This is the calling [Root: qoph resh aleph] and chirping, i.e. the prayers, that we make for that holy bird, which is Malkhut, at the beginning. Subsequently, since the remaining days Hesed, Gevurah, Tipheret, Netsach, Hod and Yesod, take hold of her, they are called 'holy convocations' in the plural. For this bird is called holy, as it is written: "For it is holy unto you" (Exodus 31:14), which is said about Malkhut, and therefore the verse uses the feminine form for 'it' [there being no neuter in Hebrew — tr.]; and because it is holy, it calls to all of them, to Hesed, Gevurah, Tipheret, Netsach, Hod and Yesod, and they come to her, which is why they are called holy convocations.

786) And she calls to Hesed, Gevurah, Tipheret, Netsach, Hod, and Yesod, and Israel chirps along with her, and they, too, call, and they therefore come to them and unite with them. This is why it is written: "These are the appointed seasons of the Lord, even holy convocations, which you shall proclaim (call) in their appointed season" (Leviticus 23:4). And they are called holy convocations after their chirping, and after that holy bird, for that which calls them is holy.

COMMENTARY:

For the secret of the verse "And the dam sitting upon the young" (Deuteronomy 22:6) is the secret of the smallness that Mother emanates to the young ones, for the first correction that Binah makes to Male and Female, namely, to Hesed, Gevurah, and Tipheret and Netsach, Hod, Yesod, and Malkhut, is the raising up of Malkhut to her. And this is the secret of the introduction of the letter yod into the light ['or: aleph waw resh] of Binah and its becoming ether [avir: aleph waw yod resh], for then Binah contracts from the force of Malkhut into the six intermediate Sephirot without the upper three Sephirot, and following her all the stages contract likewise, and they all receive the six intermediate Sephirot without the upper three Sephirot, and this is because of the ascent of Malkhut to Binah of all the stages. And this emanation is termed "And the dam sitting upon the young" (ibid.), for had Male and Female not received this smallness from Binah, they would not have been fitting to receive any intelligences (as is explained in Bereshit Aleph, page 7). And it is therefore discerned that Hesed, Gevurah, and Tipheret and Netsach, Hod, Yesod, of Ze'ir Anpin, as well as Malkhut, ascended to be under the wings of Binah, and thus receive their smallness. However, on Holy Days and festivals, Israel by their prayers and enjoyment of the festivals have to bring Malkhut and the six intermediate Sephirot of Ze'ir Anpin down from under the wings of Binah, and draw down to them intelligences of greatness from Binah.

And on the text (780): "A certain bird... and they are to be found between the wings of Mother;" i.e. Malkhut receives smallness from Mother, which is termed the wings of Mother, in the secret of Malkhut ascending to Binah, i.e. of the yod that entered the light ['or: aleph waw resh] of Binah and becoming ether [avir: aleph waw yod resh] (as above, Vayetse, 17). And the drawing down of the upper three Sephirot from Binah to Malkhut is termed hunting. And there is bad hunting, which is the secret of the verse "a cunning hunter" (Genesis 25:27), which is written about the wicked Esau, because he used to draw down the upper three Sephirot of the left side, something that it is forbidden to do. But Israel knows how to hunt well, which is the secret of drawing down the six intermediate Sephirot of Hokhmah that are singled out on the right side with hasadim by the central column. And on the text: "And Israel knows how to hunt well for good and valuable game," for the hunting of Israel is the secret of good game, and not bad game full of judgments as Esau. And it is great and valuable, i.e. it is the valuable intelligences of greatness, and this is by the unity of the left side with the right side in the central column, and by the mating of Ze'ir Anpin and Malkhut. And on the text: "What did they do? ...with slight sounds from the mouth that they whisper to her, one after the other," i.e. by their prayers they raise up the Female Waters to draw down the upper illumination in order to remove the letter yod from the ether [avir: aleph waw yod resh] of Binah, thus returning the upper three Sephirot to Binah, so that it will be able to emanate them to Malkhut. Initially, the left column of Binah emerges in the secret of the point of the shuruk (as above, Bereshit Aleph, 15), and Malkhut receives from it the illumination of Hokhmah of the left side, that is called head.

And on the text (781): "And that bird that becomes excited at those whispers ...raises her head: i.e. it emerges from the smallness of Mother, and receives the upper three Sephirot of the left side that is called head. And on the text: "And bursts out to them, emerging from under the wings of Mother," for it emerged from the smallness of Mother, but has not yet attained real greatness in the upper three Sephirot of the left side, which are the intelligences of the rear. And on the text: "So Israel takes her and holds her, whispering to her and tying her with a knot so that she will not fly off and leave." That is to say that they raise up the Female Waters by their prayers, in order to contract her from the upper three Sephirot of the left side, by means of the revelation of the Curtain of Chireq. And on the text: "holds her." For the Curtain of Chireq is the knot with which Malkhut is tied under Yesod of Ze'ir Anpin. And on the text: "Tying her with a knot so that she will not fly off

and leave," i.e. so that she should not be able to fly away and
return to the aspect of the upper three Sephirot of the left side,
for Israel has no portion there. And on the text: "Israel
immediately catches her in this knot, and the bird wants to fly
off and leave them but is unable to do so." For the Curtain of
Chireq contracts the upper three Sephirot of the left side in
such a way that it is no longer able to return to them (as
above, Lekh, 13). And on the text: "But is unable to do so."
And after Malkhut has been contracted into a point under
Yesod, it has to be raised up to the palace of Father and
Mother, where a new edifice will be constructed, in order to be
fitted for the mating with Ze'ir Anpin, face to face. And this
is the secret of the verse: "And the rib, which the Lord God
has taken from the man, made He a woman" (Genesis 2:22).
And on the text (782): "And while she is still bound in the
hands of Israel," i.e. while she is still contracted. "They whisper
their sounds," i.e. they raise up the Female Waters by their
prayers. "And flies up." She ascends to the palace of Father and
Mother to be rebuilt. "And down," she descends when she is
rebuilt and corrected, to unite frontally with Ze'ir Anpin. And
on the text: "And all those sons who are under the wings of
their mother," i.e. the six intermediate Sephirot of Ze'ir Anpin,
namely, Hesed, Gevurah, and Tipheret, Netsach, Hod, and
Yesod, that were receiving the smallness of Binah, which is
called the wings of their mother, as above. "When they hear the
chirping of their sister... and the sound of that whisper," i.e.
the sound of Israel's prayers, and the song of Malkhut, which
is the secret of the Female Waters that they raise up to Ze'ir
Anpin. "Emerge from under the wings of their mother," they
also emerge from the smallness of Mother. "And fly towards
that bird," and they fly to join Malkhut frontally. "And Israel
takes them," for they receive the intelligences of Ze'ir Anpin
and Malkhut. "And unites with them," and they become united
with them." And had it not been for that bird, with which they

were attached initially, they... would never have flown to them," for the hasadim are received from Ze'ir Anpin, and Hokhmah is received from Malkhut in the state of unity (as above, Bereshit Aleph, page 276). And so long as Israel has no Hokhmah, hasadim are understood to be received only for the aspect of the six intermediate Sephirot without the head. It is therefore essential that Hokhmah be first received from Malkhut, and subsequently hasadim can be received from Ze'ir Anpin, for they, hasadim, are the aspect of the upper three Sephirot. And it follows that: "Had it not been for that bird, with which they were attached initially," had they not first received Hokhmah from that bird, which is Malkhut. "They would never have flown to them," Hesed, Gevurah, and Tipheret, Netsach, Hod and Yesod of Ze'ir Anpin, would never have flown to Israel, for they would thus have remained the six intermediate Sephirot without the upper three. Futhermore, before Hesed, Gevurah, and Tipheret, Netsach, Hod, and Yesod of Ze'ir Anpin unite with Malkhut, they themselves contain no aspect of Hokhmah, for Ze'ir Anpin always cleaves to the upper three Sephirot of Binah, which are hidden hasadim. They are not therefore called holy convocations, where the meaning of holy is the upper three Sephirot, until after Ze'ir Anpin unites with Malkhut. And on the text (785): "And because it is holy, it calls to all of them... and they come to her." For, Netsach, Hod and Yesod, because they unite with Malkhut, they are called holy convocations, i.e. they contain the upper three Sephirot, as above.

THE FAITHFUL SHEPHERD

A BIRD'S NEST

787) The Faithful Shepherd said: How obscure these matters are for one who does not know them, and how transparent for

one who does! Certainly that bird is the Shekhinah and its nest
is the Temple, where the Shekhinah rested. And Israel are the
young ones, upon whom the dam, which is the Shekhinah, sits.
Scripture says: "And the dam sitting upon the young or upon
the eggs" (Deuteronomy 22:6). The young refer to the sages of
the Mishnah, who abound in precepts. "Or upon the eggs"
refers to the sages of the Bible.

788) But when Israel sinned, and the Temple was destroyed,
what is written? "You shall surely let the dam go" (ibid. v.7),
the dam being the Shekhinah. This is as it is written: "And for
your transgressions was your mother put away" (Isaiah 50:1).
And about the sages of the six orders of the Mishnah, it is
written: "But the young you may take for yourself"
(Deuteronomy 22:7), where "the young" refers to the six orders
of the Mishnah, from the side of the six sons Hesed, Gevurah,
and Tipheret, Netsach, Hod and Yesod, which are under upper
Mother, which is Binah, and which are alluded to in the six
words of the Shema Israel (Hear, O-Israel, the-Lord, our-God,
the-Lord, is-One.), or in the six orders of the Mishnah. It is all
the same, whether a man offers much or little, if only he
directs his mind towards Heaven (Mishnah, Menachot 13, 11),
i.e. to unite Malkhut with Ze'ir Anpin who is called Heaven,
and binds it with the knot of the phylacteries on the head and
on the arm (as is clarified below, 789).

COMMENTARY:

"Eggs" refers to the sages of the Bible, who are the secret of
the light of the soul [nephesh]. "The young" refers to the sages
of the Mishnah, who are the secret of the light of the spirit

[ruach]. And they are still in a state of smallness, without the upper three Sephirot, who are called greatness. And the kabbalists are the secret of the light of the greatness, and are called "sons." However, there is the aspect of the six intermediate stages of greatness, which is like the unity that there is in the six words of the Shema Israel (Hear, O-Israel, the-Lord, our-God, the-Lord is-one.) (As above, Terumah, 126 and Beha'alotkha, 3.) And these issued forth from the overall group of the young, which is the six intermediate Sephirot without a head, but have not yet come fully into the aspect of sons, for they have only the six intermediate stages of greatness and lack the upper three stages of greatness, and so they, too, are called sons. And on the text: "And about the sages of the six orders of the Mishnah, it is written: 'But the young you may take for yourself' (Deuteronomy 22:7)." "The young" refers to the six orders of the Mishnah, from the side of the six sons, which are under upper Mother, i.e. the six intermediate stages of greatness, upon which upper Mother already rests, but only from the aspect of the six intermediate stages. And on the text: "Which are under upper Mother... and which are alluded to in the six words of the Shema Israel." For these six intermediate stages of greatness are drawn to Ze'ir Anpin with the six words of the Shema Israel. "Or in the six orders of the Mishnah." And it follows that there are two aspects to the sages of the Mishnah, either the aspect of spirit [ruach] only, which is smallness, or the aspect of the six intermediate stages of greatness, and about them it is said: Whether a man offers much, which is the six intermediate stages of greatness, or whether he offers little, which is the light of the ordinary spirit, so long as he directs his mind toward Heaven, to the unity of Malkhut with Ze'ir Anpin that is called Heaven, it is all the same.

789) With what do the sons take the above-mentioned six intermediate stages of greatness? That is, in how many recitations of the sounds of the Shema Israel? For the six intermediate stages of greatness are drawn down in the unity of the recital of the Shema Israel, as above. And afterwards they secretly whisper the silent prayer, i.e. the Amidah (or Shemoneh Esreh) prayer to the Mother, which is Binah, in order to draw down the upper three stages of greatness to the daughter, which is Malkhut, and these are hey hey, for Mother is the first hey of the Tetragrammaton [yod hey waw and hey] and the daughter is the last hey. And they descend to the waw which is Ze'ir Anpin, with his knot, which is the yod of the Tetragrammaton [yod hey waw and hey], i.e. Hokhmah. And upper hey, which is Binah, rests upon the waw, which is Ze'ir Anpin, this being the secret of the head phylactery, i.e. the intelligences of the upper three Sephirot. And the small hey, which is Malkhut, descends to the yod of the Tetragrammaton [yod hey waw and hey], which is the knot of the upper hey that is on the head of the waw, for this is the secret of Father, which is the yod of the Tetragrammaton [yod hey waw and hey], and the secret of daughter, which is Malkhut. And this is the waw, which is Ze'ir Anpin, that is connected with her in the hey, by a faint hand, i.e. the knot of the hand phylactery. And this is in such a way that the yod of the Tetragrammaton [yod hey waw and hey], which is the secret of the knot of the head phylactery, which is the secret of Mother on the head of the waw and is the knot of the hand phylactery, which is Malkhut, is with the faint hand of Ze'ir Anpin.

790) And for this reason, the young ones are from the side of the letter waw, i.e. the light of the spirit, which includes the six orders of the Mishnah, namely Hesed, Gevurah, and Tipheret, Netsach, Hod, and Yesod. "Or upon the eggs" refers to the sages of the Bible, which are in the aspect of the light of

the soul [nephesh], which is Malkhut, the final hey of the
Tetragrammaton [yod hey waw and hey]. And it is said about
them: At five (the numerical value of hey) years old, one is fit
for the study of Scripture, (Mishnah, Pirkey Avot, 5, 21), and
this is Malkhut, which is hey. Sons refers to the side of Ben
Yah, i.e. Ze'ir Anpin, which has the upper three Sephirot from
Yah [yod hey], and these are the Kabbalists, about whom it is
said: "You shall not take the dam with the young"
(Deuteronomy 22:6).

MOSES'S BRIDE

791) And the Kabbalists are also called the sages of the
Talmud, and it is said about them: "And you shall teach them
diligently" (Deuteronomy 6:7 — part of the recital of the Shema
Israel — tr.). And the sages of the Mishnah taught: Do not read
Veshinantam ("And you shall teach them diligently") but
Veshilashtam ("And you shall divide them into three parts"),
namely, a third Bible, a third Mishnah, and a third Talmud.
(Cf. Talmud Bavli, Kiddushin 30a.) And the secret of the
matter is: "If a bird's nest chance to be before you in the way,
in any tree or on the ground" (Deuteronomy 22:6): "in the way"
refers to the sages of the Bible, "in any tree" to the sages of the
Mishnah, and "or on the ground" to the sages of the Talmud (as
above, 751), i.e. a third in Bible, a third in Mishnah, and a
third in Talmud. And one need not be surprised that the sages
changed the word Veshinantam ("And you shall teach them
diligently") into Veshilashtam ("And you shall divide them into
three parts"), for on the Scriptural verse "And you shall make a
candelabra of pure gold, of beaten work..." (Exodus 25:31),
they taught: "And you shall make a candlestick" is a general
proposition, "of gold" is a particular proposition, and "of beaten
work" is a general proposition. [This is one of the exegetical

principles by which the Torah is expounded, e.g. Two general
propositions, separated from each other by an enumeration of
particulars, include only such things as are similar to those
specified. See Boraitha d'Rabbi Ishmael and cf. Talmud Bavli,
Menachot 28b, for this instance.] And there are likewise a
number of verses where the sages of the Mishnah expand or
restrict the meaning, according to the exegetical principles of
Ribbui [according to which certain particles indicate an
inclusion or amplification — tr.] and Mi'ut [where other
particles point to a limitation, exclusion or diminution], and
there are also cases where a letter is added, as when it is said:
Do not read 'what' [mah: mem hey] but 'one hundred' [me'ah:
mem aleph hey] (See Tosephists to Talmud Bavli, Menachot
43b.) And so it is in our case when we say: Do not read
Veshinantam ("And you shall teach them diligently") but
Veshilashtam ("And you shall divide them into three parts"),
and we deduce from this: a third in the Bible, a third in the
Mishnah, and a third in the Talmud, as it is expounded in
(Talmud Bavli, Tractate) Kiddusin (30a).

792) So, too: "And it came to pass on the day that Moses had
made an end [kalot: kaph lamed waw tav] of setting up the
tabernacle" (Numbers 7:1), which we interpret as though it
were written kalat [kaph lamed tav], i.e. the kalah, bride of
Moses (above, 252) [that is to say, as though kalot were written
in the abbreviated form, without a waw — tr.]. And lest you
think that we have this exegesis from them, i.e. from the letters
of the Alphabet in the word, where the root of the word
meaning 'to make an end' [kaph lamed hey] is the same as the
word meaning 'a bride,' without adding anything (for it is not
permitted to add or take away a letter from it, nor to substitute
one letter for another, and the text in the Torah is written with
the full spelling kalot: kaph lamed waw tav, with a waw —
who, then, gave permission to take away from it, namely

the waw and to interpret it as kalat (kaph lamed tav) in the abbreviated spelling, i.e. readable as kalat, 'the bride of?' There is here no case of substitution of alphabets, e.g. Atbash, where the last letter of the alphabet, tav, is substituted for the first letter, aleph, and the penultimate letter, shin, for the second letter, beit, and so on. But rather the waw has been removed from the word, and it has been expounded as kaph lamed tav, written without the waw. But certain words that are written in the abbreviated spelling are expounded as though written out in full, and other words that are written out full are expounded as though written out in the abbreviated form. About these and about all sorts of explanations that can be made to embellish the bride, which is the Torah, in its adornments, the Holy One, blessed be He, commanded us to do as they say, and to trust them, as it is written: "According to the Torah which they will teach you" (Deuteronomy 17:11).

793) The matter may be likened to a tailor who has cut cloth in order to make royal garments, and has made many pieces from them. Those who know the places where those pieces are missing and which pieces remain will be able to make the garments, for the pieces that have been collected together are placed where they are missing, and pieces that are too small are added to. And this is the true meaning of the verse: "According to the Torah which they will teach you" (Deuteronomy 17:11).

794) And you might well ask that, if this is so, what about the case where one of them occasionally makes a mistake and says: I am sorry. The response to this is that before issuing instructions concerning that matter about which there is a difference of opinion, the one who poses the difficulty can say: I withdraw. For not all those who make the parts of a bride's adornments know where each piece goes, until the ruling is

made, and until the arguments of the halakhot (legal rulings) have been given.

795) The candelabra has seven lights which are the secret of the verse "the seven maidens, who were fitting to be given to her out of the king's house" (Esther 2:9) (that were explained above, Vayaqhel, 53), and they correspond to the three-headed shin and the four-headed shin of the phylacteries, i.e. to the seven heads of the two shins together. And these correspond to the seven blessings of the Shema Israel, namely: In the morning two blessings are said before the recital of the Shema Israel and one after, and in the evening, two blessings are said before and two after (Mishnah, Berakhot 1, 4). And subsequently is written the precept that the high priest at the Temple Service has to serve with the wings of the precept, namely bells and pomegranates (see Exodus 39:25), which are as the knots and links of the fringes and the plate which is as the phylacteries. From that point on it is written: "And you shall make an altar to burn incense on" (Exodus 30:1).

YOU SHALL PRESENT AN OFFERING MADE BY FIRE, A BURNT OFFERING

796) The Faithful Shepherd began by saying: It is written "You shall present an offering made by fire, a burnt offering to the Lord" (Numbers 28:19), and it has already been taught that a burnt offering is committed to the flames, all of it being burnt by fire, and this is why the two expressions "an offering made by fire" and "a burnt offering" are placed next to each other. And it has also been taught: A burnt offering is due only as an expiation for sinful meditation of the heart. (Cf. Midrash Rabba Leviticus 7, 3 — in the name of Rabbi Shimeon b. Yohai.)

797) Without doubt the purpose of all the sacrifices is only for
the making of atonement, with each sacrifice making
atonement for man's limbs according to the sin he committed
with that limb. For drops of marrow, i.e. the sin of wasting
seed, he brings "unleavened cakes for it was not leavened"
(Exodus 12:39); i.e. if he discharged initial drops before they
acidify in a place that does not belong to him, i.e. without a
forbidden woman in whom the drops acidify. And regarding
those that acidified, which is discharged in a place where he
should not have, i.e. in a female forbidden to him — where the
drops acidify, he has to bring leavened bread, and thus were
the thanksgiving offerings: some were leavened and others were
unleavened (see Leviticus 7:12 — 13).

798) Bullocks are from the side of Judgement. Likewise, sheep
and rams and he-goats and goats are all from the side of
Judgement, because they are 'the face of ox,' as it is said: "the
face of an ox on the left side" (Ezekiel 1:10), which is that of
Judgement. All of them were slaughtered on the north side and
their blood was received in a vessel of ministry on the north
side. The slaughtering, the receipt, and tossing (of the blood)
were all on the north side (see Mishnah, Zevachim, chapter 5),
which is the left side, in order to flavour the pill and mitigate
the attribute of Judgement, which comes to the Court from the
side of Gevurah. The Great Law-court is from the side of
Gevurah, where Binah is, while the Small Law-court is from
the side of Malkhut. And all those who shed blood in
fulfillment of a precept are from the side of Gevurah.

799) And the teaching that "the burnt-offering of each
sabbath" (Numbers 28:10) must be offered on that sabbath, and
not on any other (cf. Talmud Bavli, Shabbat 114a, bot.) is
because if the day has passed, the offering lapses (cf. Talmud
Bavli, Berakhot 26a, bot.) and it cannot be made up on another

sabbath. The offering of the sacrifice takes precedence over (the regulations of) the sabbath, and fire may be kindled on the sabbath [in order to make the burnt-offering, despite the injunction: "You shall kindle no fire throughout your habitations on the sabbath day." (Exodus 35:3) — tr.] because it is holy fire, for the fire that is used for offering all the sacrifices is holy, and this holy fire and the holy sabbath take hold of each other.

800) But profane fire may not be combined with the holy, i.e. with the sabbath, which is why He commanded Israel: "You shall kindle no fire throughout your habitations on the sabbath day" (Exodus 35:3), for this would be tantamount to mixing good and bad, for on the sabbath the Tree of Life is in control, and there is no mixture of good and bad in it. And profane matters of purity may not be mixed with the fire of holiness, and how much more so may the profane matters of impurity not be mixed with holiness. So, too, all the sacrifices are called "holy flesh" (Jeremiah 11:15), and all the sacrifices of every type contain profane things of purity, and they contain holiness, and the holy of holies.

801) And the secret of the matter is that a distinction is to be made between one holiness and another, as it is written: "And the veil shall make a division for you between the holy place and the holy of holies" (Exodus 26:33). Here, too, the fires of the offering are not equal, for the fire that is higher is more holy than the holy fire below, which are called the fire of the holy wood and the fire of the holy flesh, and in the holy fire there is a distinction as against ordinary fire that is brought to the altar, even though it has been taught that it is a positive precept to bring ordinary fire (cf. Talmud Bavli, Eruvin 63a) even when there is holy fire on the altar, for each has to have its own place.

802) Israel is likened to this, for Israel as a rule is called kings, as it has been taught: All Jews are the sons of kings (cf. Talmud Bavli, Shabbat 128a). But when they entered the Temple, each one went to his own place, the priests by themselves, the Levites by themselves, and the Israelites by themselves. Similarly, with regard to the sacrifices: although about each one it is written "a sacrifice to the Lord", they are not equal, for He, the Holy One, blessed be He, distributes everything, each as is fitting. And the secret of the matter can be learned from the fruits of the festival that Israel used to offer before the Lord, and He distributed them for the sustenance of the 70 nations.

AND IN THE DAY OF THE FIRST-FRUITS

803) Said the Holy Luminary, namely Rabbi Shimeon: Arise, O Faithful Shepherd, from your sleep, for you and the patriarchs are called "those that sleep in the dust" (see Daniel 12:2), for until now you have engaged in the Torah with those who sleep at the Mishnah, about whom it is said: This is the way to get knowledge of the Torah... and on the ground shall you sleep (Mishnah, Pirkey Avoth 6, 4). And it is said: "Also in the day of the first-fruits, when you bring a new meal offering to the Lord" (Numbers 28:26). You are the first-fruits of the Shekhinah, and through your deeds the Shekhinah is renewed in the prayers of the patriarchs each day, for the sages of the Mishnah taught: The prayers were ordained corresponding to the patriarchs, (cf. Talmud Yerushalmi, Berakhot 4, 1), and to the recital of the Shema Israel. For the Faithful Shepherd, i.e. our Teacher Moses, said: "Hear O Israel" (Deuteronomy 6:4); and it has been taught: "This book of the Torah shall not depart out of your mouth, if you shall meditate Shema Israel therein day and night" (Joshua 1:8) (Cf. Talmud Bavli, Menachot 99b — in the name of Rabbi Shimeon Bar Yohai.)

804) Certainly in your prayer and in your recital of the Shema Israel, the Shekhinah is renewed before the Holy One, blessed be He, and this is why it is said: "And you shall present a new meal offering to the Lord" (Leviticus 23:16), i.e. by the prayers which are instead of the sacrifices. But in which sacrifices, namely prayers, is (the Shekhinah) renewed? "In your (feast of) weeks" (Numbers 28:26), i.e. the Festival of Weeks, which is when the Torah was given [to Moses on Mt. Sinai — tr.], and which is called fifty days of the counting of the Omer [from the Festival of Passover — tr.], and which comprises seven weeks (see Leviticus 23:16), from the side of the One about whom it is said: "Seven times a day do I praise You" (Psalms 119, 164), which is Malkhut, which is called a bride, and is composed of the seven Sephirot Hesed, Gevurah, and Tipheret, Netsach, Hod, Yesod, and Malkhut, and is composed of Binah; and it (Malkhut) spreads out in five Sephirot Hesed, Gevurah, and Tipheret, Netsach, and Hod — into fifty.

805) Yesod, which is called All [kol: kaph lamed, 20 + 30 = 50], whose numerical value is fifty, is also composed of these fifty, namely: Hesed, Gevurah, and Tipheret, Netsach and Hod, each of which is composed of ten, and Malkhut is called bride [kalah: kaph lamed hey], the letters of which can be read as: kol [kaph lamed, meaning All] hey [having the numerical value of 5, i.e. 5 Sephirot composed of 50]. Each of them is a factor of fifty. Hokhmah, which is upper yod (numerical value 10) is a factor of 50, for 5 x 10 = 50, where hey (numerical value 5) is Binah and yod (10) is Hokhmah, and there are yod hey in Hokhmah, which, when multiplied by each other, make 50, and there are yod hey in Binah; and when yod (numerical value of 10) is multiplied by hey (numerical value of 5), the result is 50, and this is the numerical value of the word All [kol: kaph lamed, 20 + 30 = 50], as above. And the numerical value of the word Sea [yam: yod mem, 10 + 40 = 50], for Binah

is called sea, and the reference is to the Sea of the Torah, where from Binah, which is called sea, emerges the Torah, which is Ze'ir Anpin. Its origin is Keter, which is infinite. The remaining Sephirot, namely, Hesed, Gevurah, and Tipheret, Netsach, Hod, Yesod, and Malkhut, are named after it: seven seas, and since the numerical value of the word for 'sea' [yam: yod mem, 10 + 40 = 50] is fifty, it follows that in each of them there is fifty. And Malkhut is called Yam Suf (literally: The Sea of Reeds, but usually rendered: The Red Sea) because it is the end [sof] of all the seas.

806) And each one of the seven weeks (between Passover and Shavuoth) is fifty, as above: "And their meal-offering... three tenth parts for each bullock and two tenth parts for the one ram" (Numbers 28:28), making altogether five tenth parts, which are five times ten, for each tenth part is ten, and five tenth parts are fifty. And on the verse: "And their meal-offering, fine flour mingled with oil, three tenth parts for each bullock, two tenth parts for the one ram, a several tenth part for every lamb of the seven lambs" (ibid.): the seven lambs correspond to "There shall be seven complete weeks" (Leviticus 23:15) [the word used here for week is 'shabbat,' sabbath — tr.], and these are seven Malkhuts, for Malkhut is called sabbath, and each one has six days with it, namely: Hesed, Gevurah, and Tipheret, Netsach, Hod and Yesod and they, with the day of the Festival of Weeks, come to fifty.

THE DAY OF ATONEMENT

807) "And on the tenth day of this seven month you shall have a holy convocation" (Numbers 29:7), where the seventh month is Tishre, and the holy convocation referred to is the Day of Atonement, which is the tenth, which is yod (numerical value

of 10), and these are the Ten Days of Repentance [between Rosh ha-Shanah, the New Year, and Yom ha-Kippurim, the Day of Atonement — tr.], and five prayer services were ordained for it (for the Day of Atonement) in order to join the yod with the hey (numerical value of 5), i.e. Hokhmah with Binah. What is the meaning of "holy convocation?" It is to differentiate it from other days when profane work is permitted, which is why Scripture says: "You shall do no manner of work" (ibid.).

808) And those days on which normal work may be done are from the side of the Tree of Knowledge of Good and Evil, that turned from a rod into a serpent and from a serpent back into a rod, for each person according to his deeds, and this Metatron is rod, while Samael is serpent. But on this day, which is the Day of Atonement that is called holy, the Tree of Life is in control, and no devil nor evil spirit joins with it, and from its side "No evil shall sojourn with You" (Psalms 5:5), but it is throughout good. And this is why in it, in the Tree of Life, the slaves find rest and go out to freedom, and emerge from their chains.

COMMENTARY:

The weekdays are Hesed, Gevurah, and Tipheret, Netsach, Hod, and Yesod of Metatron, who is drawn down from the side of the Tree of Knowledge of Good and Evil, which is Malkhut, and therefore on weekdays, a person acts both well and badly. If he is meritorious he cleaves to Metatron, who is called rod, but, if not, he cleaves to Samael, who is wicked and is called Serpent. Thus the control over a man changes according to his deeds, this being the secret of a rod that changes into a serpent, for a man's deeds change the control over him from good to bad or vice versa. But on the Day of Atonement, which is called holy, the Tree of Life, which is Ze'ir Anpin, is in control, and this is all good, with Satan and Samael having no hold on it. And he who is privileged to cleave to the Day of Atonement, which is the secret of the Tree of Life, is already out of the rule of change from rod to serpent, and is privileged to cleave to it for eternity, and no evil has control over him anymore. And this is the secret of the verse: "No evil shall sojourn with You" (Psalms 5:5), which is said about one who is privileged to cleave to the Tree of Life. And on the text: "And go out to freedom and emerge from their chains." For they then become free men, freed of the War of Good and Evil, and they emerge forever from the chains of Evil Forces.

809) Those over whom there is a judgement, a judgement not to be changed by vow or oath, it was decreed for this reason that the following shall be recited: "All vows, bonds, etc. They shall all of them be released and annulled. They shall not be binding, nor shall they have any power." [This famous passage, the Kol Nidrei, is recited at the opening of the service on the eve of the Day of Atonement. Cf. Talmud Bavli, Nedarim 23b: One who does not wish to keep his vows during the year should stand up on the New Year and say: Let no vow that I vow hereafter be binding. Based on Ezekiel 40:1, the tenth day of the month (now called the Day of Atonement) was understood to have been called the New Year. — tr.] But the judgement shall be voided over them. And this is why the vow is in the name of the Tetragrammaton [yod hey waw and hey], which is Tipheret, while the oath is in the name of the

'The Lord' [aleph dalet nun yod], which is Malkhut, for they caused their own exile by their sins. And now, by means of Hokhmah and Binah, they will be released and annulled; they shall not be binding, nor shall they have any power, "And all the congregation of the children of Israel shall be forgiven" (Numbers 25:26). Hesed is water, Gevurah is fire, and Tipheret is ether, and since the vows are in Tipheret, which is ether [avir], the sages of the Mishnah therefore taught: (The rules about) release from vows (by resort to a sage) hover in the air [avir], for the release from Hokhmah and Binah hovers in the avir (ether), which is Tipheret, and from there annuls the vow.

810) And since the oath is from Malkhut, which is below the vow which is Tipheret, they taught that the vows are above the oaths, and they also taught: Everyone who swears an oath is as though he swears on the king himself, and everyone who vows a vow is as though he does so on the life of the king. (Cf. Talmud Bavli, Rosh ha-Shanah 17b, bot.) The king himself refers to 'The Lord' [aleph dalet nun yod], which is Malkhut. The life of the king refers to the Tetragrammaton [yod hey waw and hey], which is Ze'ir Anpin, from whom the life flows to the king, which is Malkhut. And for this reason, it is written: "When a man vows a vow to the Tetragrammaton" (Numbers 30:3), which is Ze'ir Anpin.

811) And even thus, there is another secret: The life of the king refers to Hokhmah, as it is written: "Wisdom preserves the life of him that has it" (Ecclesiastes 7:12). Therefore everyone who vows on the Tetragrammaton [yod hey waw and hey], which is Tipheret. It is as if he vowed on Hokhmah of Ze'ir Anpin, which is the Tetragrammaton in the filling of alephs, thus: yod waw dalet hey aleph waw aleph waw hey aleph, which is the life of the king, which is the life of Ze'ir Anpin. And everyone who swears an oath on the 'The Lord' [aleph

dalet nun yod] is as though he swore on the king himself. This
is because himself [atsmo] is upper Mother, i.e. Binah, and it is
as though he had sworn on her, namely, on "the like of the
very [etsem] heaven for clearness" (Exodus 24:10), namely, the
intelligences of Malkhut, for from the point of view of Hesed,
Malkhut is called "bone of my bones" (Genesis 2:23) [where the
word etsem: ayyin tsade mem, is variously rendered as self,
very, bone — tr.]. But from the point of view of Gevurah,
Malkhut is called "and flesh of my flesh" (ibid.), and in
Hokhmah, which is the life of Tipheret, i.e. its intelligences, it,
Tipheret, rises up to be called man [adam: aleph dalet mem, 1 +
4 + 40 = 45], which has the same numerical value as the
Tetragrammaton, filled in with alephs [yod-waw-dalet
hey-aleph waw-aleph-waw hey-aleph, 10 + 6 + 4 + 5 + 1 + 6 +
1 + 6 + 5 + 1 = 45], as it is written: "Man is as Tipheret"
(Isaiah: 44). For Tipheret is called man when it has the
intelligences of Hokhmah, which is the secret of the
Tetragrammaton filled in with alephs, that has the numerical
value of 45.

812) And it is said about the Day of Atonement: "And you
shall afflict your souls" (Numbers 29:7) and also: "In the seventh
month on the tenth day of the month, you shall afflict your
souls" (Leviticus 16:29). And five afflictions were decreed for
it, so that small hey (numerical value 5), which is Malkhut,
should be purified in upper hey, which is Binah, from which
the afflictions are drawn down, i.e. from its left column. And
they are five prayers [Evening, Morning, Additional,
Afternoon, and Closing recited on the Day of Atonement —
tr.], to establish in Israel: "Though your sins be as scarlet, they
shall be as white (purified) as snow" (Isaiah 1:18). And this is
the secret of the thread of crimson wool which used to be tied
to the door of the Sanctuary from inside. And when the
he-goat reached the wilderness, the thread turned white
(Mishnah, Yoma, 6, 7). All the iniquities of the House of Israel

reach Malkhut, and Repentance, which is Binah, purifies
(whitens) them, for it is written about it, about Malkhut: I am
the Lord "that dwells with them in the midst of their
uncleanness" (Leviticus 16:16), and the four garments of white
and the four garments of gold for apparel are the secret of yod
aleph hey dalet waw nun hey yod, which is the combination of
the letters of the Tetragrammaton [yod hey waw and hey] and
those of 'The Lord' [aleph dalet nun yod], for the four
garments of white are the secret of the four letters of the
Tetragrammaton [yod hey waw and hey] while the four
garments of gold are the secret of the four letters of 'The Lord'
[aleph dalet nun yod].

813)   And it was decreed that a shophar (ram's horn) be
sounded on the Day of Atonement, to raise up a voice, which
is the letter waw of the Tetragrammaton [yod hey waw and
hey], i.e. Ze'ir Anpin, for freedom, which is Binah. For it is
said about it: "In all their affliction he was afflicted" (Isaiah
63:9) [literally: In all their affliction was affliction for him].
The word in this verse for "for him" is lo, lamed waw, which is
how it is to be read, although what is written is lo,' lamed
aleph, meaning 'no,' or 'not.' For "In all their affliction" (ibid.)
alludes to five afflictions, and the judgments whose source is
in Binah, in its left column. And in the secret of the shophar
blowing, Ze'ir Anpin is also raised up there to Binah, and this
is why there are two versions of the text, as written and as
read, with an aleph and with a waw, where the aleph alludes to
Binah, in the secret of aleph Binah, and the waw alludes to
Ze'ir Anpin that ascended to Binah. And the worship of the
Day of Atonement is conducted at length and comprises three
stages: thought, speech, and deed.

THE FESTIVALS OF BOOTHS

814)   "And on the fifteenth day of the seventh month you shall
have a holy convocation; you shall do no manner of servile

work, and you shall keep a feast to the Lord seven days"
(Numbers 29:12). On the fifteenth day means from the side of
yod hey (numerical values: 10, 5), namely, Hokhmah and
Binah. The seventh month; this is Tishre. "And you shall keep a
feast;" this is the letters of the letter waw, which is the central
column, i.e. Ze'ir Anpin. Seven days is from the side of Bat
Sheva (the daughter of seven), which is Malkhut, which is the
last hey (of the Tetragrammaton). The patriarchs which are
Hesed, Gevurah, and Tipheret, and the Faithful Shepherd who
is Netsach, and Aaron who is Hod, and David who is Malkhut,
and Solomon [Shlomoh] who is Yesod that is called shalom
(peace) are seven, corresponding to seven Sephirot. I want to
construct for you a succah (booth or tabernacle), which is
upper Mother, that will provide a roof over them, over the
seven Sephirot, as the dam over the young.

815) And on account of the seven Sephirot, Scripture said:
"For I made the Children of Israel to dwell in booths, when I
brought them out of the Land of Egypt" (Leviticus 23:43), i.e.
with seven clouds of glory, which are the secret of seven
Sephirot. The word succah (booth or tabernacle) when written
with a letter waw, in the full spelling (i.e. samekh waw kaph
hey), is in the secret of the two sons, over whom Binah
provides a cover, namely, the Tetragrammaton [yod hey waw
and hey] and 'The Lord' [aleph dalet nun yod], i.e. Ze'ir Anpin
and Malkhut, for the numerical value of succah [samekh waw
kaph hey, 60 + 6 + 20 + 5 = 91] is the same as that of yod
aleph hey dalet waw nun hey yod (10 + 1 + 5 + 4 + 6 + 50 + 5
+ 10 = 91) (this being the combination of the Tetragrammaton
and 'The Lord'), for succah [samekh waw kaph hey] consists of
the letters kaph waw (20 + 6 = 26), which have the same
numerical value as the letters of the Tetragrammaton [yod hey
waw and hey, 10 + 5 + 6 + 5 = 26], and the letters samekh hey
(60 + 5 = 65) which have the same numerical value as 'The

Lord' [aleph dalet nun yod, 1 + 4 + 50 + 10 = 65], and they are
the secret of the two cherubs who are "screening the ark-cover
with their wings, with their faces one to another" (Exodus
25:20), and this is the secret of Ze'ir Anpin and Malkhut.

816) And the cherubs, who are Male and Female, are ten
handsbreadth from the bottom to the top, i.e. ten Sephirot of
reflected light, from their feet to their heads, and ten Sephirot
of direct light from their heads to their feet, and they rest on a
handbreadth, which is the secret of yod (whose numerical value
is ten). They therefore contain ten from top to bottom and ten
from bottom to top, i.e. the ten Sephirot of direct light and the
ten Sephirot of reflected light, and this is yod, written out in
full: yod waw dalet, whose numerical sum is (10 + 6 + 4 =) 20.
And this is why the rabbis ruled that the size of a succah
should be not less than ten and not more than twenty (cf.
Talmud Bavli, Succah 2a). A succah that is built in the shape
of a furnace is from the side of Mother, which is Judgement,
about which it is said: "Now Mount Sinai was altogether on
smoke, because the Lord descended on it in fire, and the smoke
thereof ascended as the smoke of a furnace" (Exodus 19:18),
and it is all one.

817) "And a tabernacle shall be for a shadow in the day-time"
(Isaiah 4:6). This is because roofing material is needed, and this
casts a shadow, about which it is said: "abiding in the shadow
of the Almighty" (Psalms 91:1). And the meaning is not to the
shadow cast by an ordinary succah that protects the body from
the sun, but to the shadow that casts a protection over the soul
[neshamah]. This is in the secret of the verse "Under its shadow
I delighted to sit" (Song of Songs 2:3) and "Of whom we said:
'Under His shadow we will live among the nations'"
(Lamentations 4:20). The word tsel (shadow) with a letter mem
added to it forms the word tselem (image), where tsel is the

secret of the roofing material and the mem is the secret of the four side-walls of the succah, and it is said: "Surely man walks as a mere image [tselem]" (Psalms 39:7). Closed (or final) mem has four sides to it, which are the secret of the four side-walls of the succah.

818) And with regard to the teaching: Two according to the regulations, and a third of even a handbreadth; and of him who says three according to the regulations, and a fourth of even a handsbreadth (cf. Talmud Bavli, Succah 6b): that is because of the three measurements, two, three, four, which together make nine, where two are Hokhmah and Binah, three are Hesed, Gevurah, and Tipheret, and four are Netsach, Hod, Yesod, and Malkhut. And the handbreadth that they mentioned with the two or with the three is the tenth, namely, Malkhut, that makes up every shortage. And this is why the size of a succah is not less than ten (handsbreadth), referring to Malkhut, which is the tenth of all the Sephirot, and not more than twenty (cubits), which is kaph (the numerical value of which is 20), that alludes to upper Keter (initial letter: kaph), which is further than the eye can see and is unfathomable. This is that upper glory, about which Moses said: "Show me, I pray You, Your glory" (Exodus 33:18), to which the Holy One, blessed be He, responded: "You cannot see My face" (ibid. v.20), and there is no glory without kaph.

819) And for this reason the sages of the Mishnah viewed as corresponding to them: a succah made like an alleyway, which is from the side of the letter beit, and like a g'am, which is from the side of the letter gimmel, and like a hut which is from the side of the letter dalet; and these seven letters — beit, gimmel, dalet, kaph, peh, resh, and tav — which are doubled by the addition of a dagesh (a dot) in them, allude to the seven Sephirot — Hesed, Gevurah, and Tipheret, Netsach, Hod,

Yesod and Malkhut, i.e. to the aspect of Judgement that is in them, and they are the initial letters that allude to the seven invalid succahs, because of the judgement that is in them. The letter kaph alludes to a succah made like a furnace (kivshan), and the beit to a succah that is a wayside station (burganin), and the other letters to the remaining invalid succahs, all of which are referred to by the sages of the Mishnah, such as the succah of fruit watchmen, the succah of shepherds, or the succah of Samaritans, etc. (Talmud Bavli, Succah 8b), and there is no need to prolong the discussion on them.

820) And corresponding to them, to the seven letters beit, gimmel, dalet, kaph, peh, resh, and tav, are the seven planets, and they are male and female, for when these seven letters are soft they are with the male and when they are hard (with a dagesh) they are with the female. And they are therefore called the seven doubles and are like the seven candles of the candlestick, which are the secret of the seven Sephirot Hesed, Gevurah, and Tipheret, Netsach, Hod, Yesod and Malkhut, and it is said about it (the candlestick): "Seven times a day do I praise You" (Psalms 119:164), and so it is said: "There are seven pipes, even seven" (Zechariah 4:2), which are the secret of the seven doubles, namely, the seven letters in their soft form and the seven letters in their hard form, and likewise, the seven Sephirot are double, containing seven of Judgement and seven of Mercy. And so, too, are the seven days of creation below, i.e. the seven Sephirot of Malkhut which are harsh with Judgments, and the seven above, i.e. the seven Sephirot of Ze'ir Anpin, which are free of Judgments. For about the seven Sephirot that are below, it is said: "There is nothing new under the sun" (Ecclesiastes 1:9), for all innovations come from the sun, namely the seven Sephirot of Ze'ir Anpin and not from 'under the sun,' by which is meant the seven Sephirot of Malkhut.

821) Lulav [one of the four species of plants used at the
Festival of Succot — tr.] is Righteous One, namely, Yesod, for
the lulav (palm-branch) is like the spinal chord that contains
eighteen vertebrae, corresponding to the 18 shaking movements
with the lulav. And they correspond to the 18 blessings of the
Amidah prayer (Shemoneh Esreh), and they correspond to the
18 times that the Divine Name, i.e. the names of the
Tetragrammaton, is mentioned in "Ascribe unto the Lord, O
sons of might" (Psalms 29), and the 18 times that the Divine
Name is mentioned in the recital of the Shema Israel. And the
Lulav is shaken in six directions: south, north, east, up, down
and west, which makes six, and it is shaken three times in each
direction, making a total of 18.

822) The lulav is taken in the right hand, and is comprised of
six, namely three myrtles, corresponding to Gedulah, Gevurah,
and Tipheret, and they are like the three colors to be found in
the eye, which are white, red, and green. And the two willow
leaves are Netsach and Hod, and they are similar to the two
lips. The lulav (palm-branch) is Yesod and is like the spinal
column that supports all the bones and about which David said:
"All my bones shall say: Lord, who is like You" (Psalms 35:10).
And the Etrog is Malkhut and is like the heart, in which are
thoughts.

823) And the shakings of the Hallel [the group of Psalms,
113-118, that are recited on festivals — tr.] are common to the
shakings of the taking up of the lulav, and there are 18
shakings at "We beseech You, O Lord, save now" (Psalms
118:25), 18 each at the first and last "O, give thanks" (ibid. v.1
and v.29), and 18 at the taking up of the lulav, making a total
of 72 shakings. And this is why the numerical value of lulav
[lamed waw lamed beit, 30 + 6 + 30 + 2 = 68], together with
the 4 of the four species that make up the lulav, comes to 72,

and this is the same as the numerical value of Hesed [chet samekh dalet, 8 + 60 + 4 = 72], which is the right arm. And this is why it was decreed that the lulav be taken in the right hand, which is the side of Hesed, and the Etrog to the side of Gevurah, to the left, corresponding to the heart. And this is why it was decreed that the Etrog, which is like the heart, be held in the left hand, as it has been taught: Lulav in the right hand and Etrog in the left, corresponding to Zahor V'Shamor (Exodus 20:8 and Deut. 5:12) one taking both Luvav and Etrog becomes a central column.

824) The patriarchs came with the Faithful Shepherd and Aaron, David, and Solomon and blessed him, Rabbi Shimeon, saying to him: You, Holy Luminary, and your companions, who are six in number, correspond to these seven Sephirot, and you, the Holy Luminary, are a westerly light in the middle of the six lights that illuminate from you. And about each one it is said: "The soul of man is the lamp of the Lord" (Proverbs 20:27). And the Faithful Shepherd illuminates through you, and you and your companions are all of you one, without any separation whatsoever. And from there and onwards, the branches, i.e. the lights, spreads out, to all the sages. Complete what you are saying in the first part, to encrown the matters.

825) The Holy Luminary began by quoting: "Many waters cannot quench love, neither can the floods drown it; if a man would give all the substance of his house for love, he would be utterly contemned" (Song of Songs 8:7) What is the meaning of "he would be utterly contemned"? This refers to the second day, the sixth day, and the seventh day of the festival of Succot (Tabernacles) on which libations of water and wine were poured out. [The Hebrew root 'contemned' is boz: beit waw zayyin, which letters have the numerical values of 2, 6, and 7, respectively — tr.]

826) During the seven days of the Festival of Succot, Israel

used to sacrifice seventy bullocks to make atonement for the 70 angels of the 70 nations, so that the world would not remain destroyed because of them. (Cf. Talmud Bavli, Succah, 55b.) And this is what the Scripture says: "And on the fifteenth day... you shall present a burnt-offering, an offering made by fire, of a sweet savor unto the Lord: thirteen young bullocks... without blemish... And on the second day... 12 young bullocks... And on the third day eleven bullocks... And on the fourth day ten bullocks... And on the fifth day nine bullocks... And on the sixth day eight bullocks... And on the seventh day seven bullocks" (Numbers 29: verses 12, 13, 17, 20, 23, 26, 29, 32). And all told, seventy bullocks were offered, each day one less being presented. Why was there a reduction of one each day?

827) And the answer to this question is that the Scripture here gives us a hint. "And the ark rested in the seventh month" (Genesis 8:4), which is Tishre. And just as then in the days of the Flood, when the waters decreased continually, so also here, in Tishre, which is the seven month, in which there are a number of precepts, the New Year and the Day of Atonement, succah, lulav and etrog, the types of lulav and shophar. For then the upper Shekhinah rests on Israel, and this is Repentance, i.e. Binah that is called Repentance, and is the secret of succah. And etrog, which is Malkhut, and lulav, that is the Holy One, blessed be He, i.e. Ze'ir Anpin, immediately "And the waters decreased continually" (Genesis 8:5), for the sins of Israel become less. So, too, the angels of destruction who are appointed over them, over the iniquities, become less, for the iniquities are similar to the waters of the Flood. As has been taught: He that commits one transgression 'gets for himself one accuser (Mishnah, Pirkey Avoth 4, 11). And at the time that the iniquities become less, their bullocks are reduced in number, the appointees over the seventy nations are reduced, the seventy nations are reduced, and their goodness becomes less.

828) And the Holy One, blessed be He, commanded Noach to take into the ark two and two, seven and seven (see Genesis 7:2), male and female, to be a sacrifice to protect Noach and all those who went into the ark with him. So, too, those who observe festivals and seasons, which are feast days, are two and two, seven and seven. Two and two refers to the two days of the New Year and the two days of the Feast of Weeks, and because these two of the Feast of Weeks are because of doubt [as to which of them is the correct date for the festival — tr.], therefore, there are two days of Purim in their stead. Seven and seven refer to the seven days of Passover, and the seven days of the Feast of Tabernacles [succot]. Noach corresponds to the sabbath day, and this is the meaning of what is written: "Of every living thing" (Genesis 6:19), because $2 + 2 + 7 + 7 = 18$, which is $8 + 10$, i.e. chet yod: chay, life.

829) The succah (tabernacle, booth) protects Israel, as it is written: "And there shall be a succah for a shadow in the day-time from the heat, and for a refuge and for a cover from storm and from rain" (Isaiah 4:6) Just as the purpose of Noach's ark was to give protection, so is the succah to give protection. Again: "Of every living thing" (Genesis 6:19), where "living" is chay: chet yod, $8 + 10 = 18$, is the 18 blessings of the prayer (the Shemoneh Esreh), which sub-divide into two groups of nine each. And with Birkat ha-Minim [the paragraph making reference to apostates and slanderers — tr.], the ten Sephirot are completed, for this makes ten together with the first nine, and again together with the last nine. And they correspond to the ten Sephirot of direct light that is from above downwards, and the ten Sephirot of reflected light that is from below upwards. And this corresponds to Noach, which is to say that the 18 blessings of the prayer (the Shemoneh Esreh) correspond to the 18 of Noach, namely, two and two, seven and seven, which add up to eighteen.

830) Again: "Of every living thing" (Genesis 6:19). This means that the Shekhinah protects all those who keep the yod which is the sign of the sabbath, in its limits, namely, eight thousand cubits, i.e. two thousand in each direction. And the yod of the sign of the sabbath and the chet (=8) of the limits are chet yod: chay, life. Again: "Of every living thing" (ibid.). This means those who keep the sign of the covenant [i.e. circumcision — tr.], which is after eight days, about which it is said: "And in the eighth day the flesh of his foreskin shall be circumcised" (Leviticus 12:3). And the yod of the sign of the covenant and the chet of the 8 days form chet yod: chay, life. Again: "Of every living thing" (ibid.) refers to those who observe the sign of the phylacteries, which is yod, and in which are eight sections, thus: chet yod: chay, life.

831) The Shekhinah, which is the succah (booth, tabernacle,), protects them and spreads her wings over them, as does the mother bird over the young. And this is why the text of the prayer was worded: Who spreads the tabernacle of peace over us [concluding line of the Hashkivenu, the second blessing after the recital of the Shema Israel at evening services — tr.]. And for this reason, in the seventh month, which contains all these precepts, "Many waters cannot quench the love" (Song of Songs 8:7) of Israel for their Father who is in Heaven. And there is no meaning to 'many waters' except all the nations and their ministers. (Cf. Midrash Song of Songs VIII, 7.) And if a man, this being Samael, give all that he possesses in this world (cf. Song of Songs 8:7) in order to join with Israel in these precepts, "He would utterly be contemned" (ibid.).

THE EIGHTH DAY OF SOLEMN ASSEMBLY

832) "On the eighth day you shall have a solemn assembly

...but you shall present... one bullock, one ram" (Numbers
29:35- 36). The sages of the Mishnah have already taught that
the matter is to be likened to the case of a king who invites
guests to his house, and after he has sent them on their way,
says to the members of his household: Let us, you and I, make
a small banquet. (Cf. Talmud Bavli, Succah, 55b.) And what is
the meaning of 'solemn assembly' [atseret: ayyin tsade resh
tav]? It is as is written: "This same shall have authority
[ya'atsor: yod ayyin tsade resh] over My people" (I Samuel
9:17). And there is no authority [ayyin tsade resh] apart from
Malkhut. For from the point of view of upper Shekhinah,
which is Binah, did he make the large banquet, but he made
the small banquet from the point of view of Malkhut. And
Israel makes joy with her, and she is called Simchat Torah, the
Rejoicing of the Torah. And the scrolls of the Torah have their
crowns placed on them, alluding to the fact that the scroll of
the Torah is Tipheret, while the Shekhinah is its crown, i.e. the
diadem of Tipheret.

833) Rabbi Elazar asked, Father, why is it that from the side
of upper Mother, which is Binah, He invited all the appointees
of all the nations, i.e. with the seventy bullocks, referred to
above, and from the side of the lower Shekhinah, He invited
only a solitary nation, corresponding to the one bullock [that is
offered on the eighth day of solemn assembly — tr.]. Should it
not have been the other way around, with Israel receiving from
upper Mother, and the ministers of the nations from Malkhut?

834) He replied: My son, that is a good question that you have
asked, and the answer is: Because Malkhut alludes to a daughter
who is modest in the house of her father and mother, and she
is engaged but not married, and it is not proper that she should
eat with the guests. But as for Mother, who is married, it is the
way of the world that when her husband invites guests, she eats

with the guests, at the table with her husband. And if they are
foreign guests, than no-one eats with them, neither father nor
mother, and certainly not the daughter, who is Malkhut. And
this is the reason why at the banquet for the seventy ministers
not one of the members of the king's household joins in to eat
with them, because they are foreigners. He (Elazar) said: Surely
the matter has now been harmonized in my thoughts correctly.

COMMENTARY:

We have here at the Festival of Tabernacles two kinds of
guests. There are the guests of the succah, which are the secret
of the seven attributes of holiness, and there are the seventy
ministers who receive the seventy bullocks. And both of them
receive from the side of upper Mother, which is Binah and not
Malkhut. And the reason for this is that Binah is married to
Father, who is Hokhmah, and she is thoroughly perfect, such
that she does eat with the guests, namely, the guests of the
succah. But Malkhut is engaged but not married, for although
she has copulations with Ze'ir Anpin, these are not from the
aspect of herself but rather from the aspect of what she
borrows from Mother (as is explained in the Introduction to
Sepher ha-Zohar, page 20); and from the aspect of herself she
is unmarried until the completion of the correction, for then
the aspect of herself is revealed and she mates with Ze'ir
Anpin. Thus, she is unable to emanate to the holy guests, and
even less so to the foreign guests, namely, the seventy
ministers. And on the text: "Because Malkhut alludes to a
daughter who is modest in the house of her father and mother."
For all her wherewithal is from Father and Mother. In the
aspect of herself she is hidden within Father and Mother. "And
she is engaged but not married." For herself she has no mating

prior to the completion of the correction. "It is not proper that she should eat with the guests." For she has to be hidden and covered with the tools of Mother, and not be revealed. "But as for Mother etc." She is thoroughly perfect, and all the emanations that there are in the worlds over six thousand years comes from her, and she, is therefore, revealed to the guests. However, to the seventy ministers, Mother is not revealed, but gives them sustenance in an aspect that is continually being reduced because they are foreign and alien to holiness, wanting to draw Hokhmah downwards from above. And therefore, after the seven days of the Festival of Tabernacles, they are rejected, and He then makes a small banquet for the members of His household from the aspect of Malkhut. And although she is even then also modest in the tools of Mother, nevertheless, since from this mating herself of Malkhut receives its correction, she is therefore called after her. And the meaning of these matters you will be able to understand from what is explained above (Tsav, page 43, which should be well studied).

EXPLANATIONS OF MALKHUT

835) The daily burnt-offering [olat tamid] is the Shekhinah which always [tamid] ascends [olah] on that stage about which it is said: 'Evening and morning, every day, always' and 'twice say (in love) Shema Israel' [Additional Service for sabbaths, in the Kedushah, the third blessing of the Shemoneh Esreh, during the reader's repetition thereof, Sephardi text — tr.]. And she ascends in the central column, which is Ze'ir Anpin, who is with her always, without any separation at all.

836) But whence does she ascend? To the place from which she was taken, which is the Infinite One, and she is then higher

than all the Sephirot, which is why it was taught: The whole of the burnt-offering ascends to the Most High. And as she ascends, all the other Sephirot take hold of her, and ascend with her. What is the meaning of this ascent of hers to the Infinite One? It is to provide a sweet savor, to give a good savor before the Lord. And afterwards it is said about her: "And he came down from offering the sin-offering and the burnt-offering" (Leviticus 9:22), i.e. she descends from the Infinite One, full of atonement over all of Israel's sins.

837) And her ascent is with the central column, which is Ze'ir Anpin, and so also is her descent, and that of all her hosts, in it. And for this reason she is called a ladder for all the appellatives; i.e. all the stages ascend and descend in her, hanging from the name of the Tetragrammaton, which is Ze'ir Anpin, and thus all the sacrifices and all the burnt-offerings are "To the Tetragrammaton." And she is called a sacrifice because all the appellatives draw near, through her, to the Tetragrammaton, which is Ze'ir Anpin.

838) And for this reason it was said about her: "And his offering was one silver dish" (Numbers 7:13), namely Malkhut. For there is no stage that can draw near to the Tetragrammaton without Malkhut, and there is no prayer, nor precept of any of the precepts that are in the Torah or any of the sacrifices and burnt-offerings that are without Malkhut. And in all the stages that are in the Sephirot, none is received before the Tetragrammaton without her, which is why it was said about her: "With this [zot, the feminine form — tr.] shall Aaron come into the holy place" (Leviticus 16:3), where Malkhut is called zot, this. And for this reason the prophet said: "But let him that glories glory in this" [zot, the feminine form — tr.]. (Jeremiah 9:23).

839) And she, Malkhut, is called peace-offerings [shelamim, from the root: shin lamed mem] because she is the completion [hashlamah, from the root: shin lamed mem] of the name of the Tetragrammaton in every stage. She is hey of the Tetragrammaton [yod hey waw and hey]; she is the 'The Lord' [aleph dalet nun yod]; she is the yod of the Tetragrammaton [yod hey waw and hey]; she is the hey of God [elohim: aleph lamed hey yod mem]; she is the hey of 'I am' [ehyeh: aleph hey yod hey]; she is the yod of Almighty [Shadday: shin dalet yod]; she is the end of every Tetragrammaton and appellative, wherefore it is said about her: "The end of the matter, all having been heard: fear God and keep His commandments" (Ecclesiastes 12:13). She is the end of the ten Sephirot and is called Yam Suf [literally: The Sea of Reeds, but usually understood: The Red Sea. Suf can be read as sof, end — tr.] (As above, 805.) She is the completion of the upper beings and of the lower beings; she is the gate by which one has to enter for all Hokhmah (wisdom) and for every appellative and Tetragrammaton, and for entering into any of the Sephirot. She is the knowledge of everything, and without her no creature has permission to look into any knowledge that is in the world. About her it is said: "This is the gate of the Lord; the righteous shall enter into it" (Psalms 118:20).

840) She, Malkhut, is the 42-letter Name, i.e. the four letters of the Tetragrammaton [yod hey waw and hey], the ten letters of the filling [where the letters of the Tetragrammaton are written out by name: yod = yod waw dalet (3); hey = hey aleph (2); waw = waw aleph waw (3); hey = hey aleph (2) — tr.], and the 28 letters of the filling of the filling [where the written-out letters of Tetragrammaton are themselves written out by name. Thus, the first letter of the Tetragrammaton, yod, becomes: yod waw dalet, waw aleph waw, dalet lamed tav (9); the second letter, hey, becomes: hey aleph aleph lamed peh (5); the third

letter waw, becomes: waw aleph waw, aleph lamed peh, waw aleph waw (9); and the fourth letter, hey, becomes: hey aleph, aleph lamed peh (5), and 9 + 5 + 9 + 5 = 28 letters]. And the four letters of the Tetragrammaton, the ten letters of the filling, and the twenty-eight letters of the filling of the filling come to forty-two letters, and Malkhut is the secret of the final heys that are in the 42-letter Name, through which the upper and lower beings were created. She is called 'eye' from the right side, which is the Hokhmah in her, as it is written: "Behold the eye of the Lord is toward them that fear Him" (Psalms 33:18); and she is called 'ear' from the left side, which is the Binah in her, as it is written: "O my God, incline Your ear and hear" (Daniel 9:18). And from the point of view of the central column, which is the Tipheret in her, she is called 'smell,' while from the aspect of herself, which is Malkhut, she is called 'mouth,' as it is written: "With him do I speak mouth to mouth" (Numbers 12:8).

841) And she is called the first of the Ten Commandments, "I am the Lord your God, who brought you out of the land of Egypt, out of the house of bondage" (Exodus 20:2), i.e. the beginning of the divine revelation, from the point of view of Keter, which is ayin (nihility), i.e. the letters aleph yod nun from Our God [eloheynu: aleph lamed hey yod nun waw], for Keter is called ayin (nihility) in the sense of absence of perception. 'I' is anokhi: aleph nun kaph yod, which contains the letter kaph that stands for Keter and the letters aleph yod nun [ayin]. And Keter is so called from the point of view of upper Mother [Binah], for whom the Exodus from Egypt is mentioned fifty times in the Torah, corresponding to the fifty gates of Binah (as above, Yitro, 389) and Keter of Malkhut is in Binah. And she is a daughter [bat: beit tav] from "In the beginning" [Breshit: beit resh aleph shin yod tav — Genesis, chapter 1], which includes all of the ten statements by which

the world was created [i.e. the tenfold "And God said" in the Biblical account of the Creation, and cf. Mishnah Pirkey Avoth 5, 1 — tr.]. And from the point of view of Hokhmah, she is bat yod [literally: the daughter of ten — tr.], as it is said: "By wisdom [hokhmah] He founded the earth" (Proverbs 3:19), i.e. Malkhut, which is called earth, for Father, which is Hokhmah, founded the daughter, which is Malkhut. And she is "the path that no bird of prey knows" (Job 28:7), which is comprised of 32 paths, namely the 32 Names of God from the point of view of upper Mother that is called glory [kavod: kaph beit waw dalet, 20 + 2 + 6 + 4 = 32], and when they are included in the daughter, which is Malkhut, Malkhut is called heart [lev: lamed beit, 30 + 2 = 32], and this is why there is glory above and heart below (as above, 711).

842) And the Ten Commandments were given on two tablets, five on each, and Malkhut includes them, for they are the five Sephirot from Keter to Gevurah [Keter, Hokhmah, Binah, Hesed, and Gevurah], and the five Sephirot from the central column, which is Tipheret to the daughter, which is Malkhut [Tipheret, Netsach, Hod, Yesod, and Malkhut], and they are twice hey (whose numerical value is 5). A question arises here: If the Ten Commandments are from the ten Sephirot, is it then possible to speak with ten mouths, with each Sephirah speaking with its own special mouth? The answer to this is that He included all Ten Commandments in the only daughter, which is Malkhut, and all of them became one, with the Ten Commandments being incorporated within Malkhut. And so it is that waw, which is Tipheret, that is called voice, cannot be perceived until it joins with speech, which is Malkhut. And this is why it is written: "You heard the voice of words" (Deuteronomy 4:12), where voice alludes to Ze'ir Anpin and words to Malkhut.

843) She, Malkhut, is the second commandment from the side of Gevurah [gimmel beit waw resh hey, 3 + 2 + 6 + 200 + 5 = 216], which is the same numerical sum as for the word 'fear', yir'ah [yod resh aleph hey, 10 + 200 + 1 + 5 = 216], and this is intimated in the word "Breshit" (In the beginning, Genesis 1:1) [Beit resh aleph shin yod tav], whose letters, re-arranged, spell: Yere' boshet (fearful of shame) [yod resh aleph beit shin tav], and it has been taught: Whoever has no modesty, certainly his forefathers were not present on Mount Sinai (at the giving of the Torah to Moses) (Cf. Talmud Bavli, Nedarim 20a.)

844) She is the third commandment, which is called "the love of kindness" (Mikhah 6:8), as it is written: "I have loved you with an everlasting love; therefore with kindness have I drawn you" (Jeremiah 31:3). Love, which is Malkhut, is composed of the patriarchs, and in their contexts is called: ba-kol, mikol, kol, which is Malkhut that is called kol (All). About Abraham it is said: "And the Lord had blessed Abraham in all things" [ba-kol] (Genesis 24:1); and about Isaac it is written: "And I have eaten of all" [mikol](ibid. 27:33); and about Jacob: "Because I have all [kol]" (ibid. 33:11). And the secret of the matter is the verse: "I remember you for the affection of your youth, the love of your espousals" (Jeremiah 2:2), which is said about Malkhut.

845) And she is the fourth commandment, which is the unity from the point of view of the central column, i.e. the unity of the Shema Israel, and she is kaph hey (20 + 5 = 25) kaph hey (20 + 5 = 25) letters with Him, with Ze'ir Anpin, i.e. the 24 letters of the Shema Israel, which is Ze'ir Anpin, and the 24 letters of (the silent response): Blessed be the Name of the glory of His kingdom forever and ever, which is Malkhut, in the six words of the Shema Israel (Hear, O-Israel, the-Lord, our-God, the-Lord is-one), which are six Sephirot of Ze'ir

Anpin; and for her sake, Abraham said: "I and the lad will go yonder [koh: kaph hey, 20 + 5 = 25], and we will worship" (Genesis 22:5), and it is also said: "Thus [koh: kaph hey, 25] shall you say to the House of Jacob" (Exodus 19:3).

846) And He, Ze'ir Anpin, is the aleph chet of one [echad: aleph chet dalet], which is the central column, while she, Malkhut, is the dalet of one [echad: aleph chet dalet]. She is the completion of His unity, perfecting him in the secret of echad. Aleph chet (1 + 8 = 9) includes nine Sephirot, namely: aleph (=1) is the Infinite One, i.e. Keter, (while chet is) the eight Sephirot from Hokhmah to Yesod [Hokhmah, Binah, Hesed, Gevurah, Tipheret, Netsach, Hod, and Yesod]. The dalet of echad [aleph chet dalet] is Malkhut, with the tip of the dalet alluding to Yesod. With it, Malkhut, are completed the ten Sephirot, which are the ten letters (of the Tetragrammaton filled in with alephs): yod waw dalet, hey aleph, waw aleph waw, hey aleph. The dalet of echad [aleph chet dalet] is comprised of the four letters of the Tetragrammaton [yod hey waw and hey].

847) The fifth commandment is: "But you shall meditate therein day and night" (Joshua 1:8). She, Malkhut, is the Written Torah from the side of Hesed and the Oral Torah from the side of Gevurah, where Hokhmah and Binah are in them, for at the time of greatness, Hesed ascends and becomes Hokhmah, while Gevurah ascends and becomes Binah. This is as the sages of the Mishnah taught: He who wants to be wise will face south and he who wants to be rich will face north (cf. Baba Batra 25b), where the meaning of rich is in knowledge and understanding, Da'at and Binah. And the central column, which is Tipheret, incorporates both of them, the right side and the left side, and for this reason is called heavens [shamayim: shin mem yod mem] for it includes fire [esh: aleph

shin] and water [mayim: mem yod mem]. (Cf. Midrash Bereshit
R a b b a 4, 7.) F i r e is G e v u r a h a n d w a t e r is H e s e d.

848) And for this reason, Keter, which is kaph (apiece), is the
secret of the verse: "weighing ten shekels apiece after the
shekel of the sanctuary" (Numbers 7:86), i.e. ten Sephirot from
above downwards and ten Sephirot from below upwards, which
is yod hey hey, three letters that become kaph, i.e. Keter, over
w a w which is Ze'ir Anpin, and is to correspond to Keter
Torah, the crown of the Torah, for the waw is the scroll of the
Torah, and the kaph, which is yod hey hey, is the diadem of
its head. And all of it together, i.e. yod hey hey with waw, is
the Tetragrammaton [yod hey waw and hey] whose numerical
value is (10 + 5 + 6 + 5 =) 26, where the kaph (whose
numerical value is 20) is the secret of Keter (crown) over the
waw (whose numerical value is 6).

COMMENTARY:

When Malkhut becomes a crown [Keter] over Ze'ir Anpin, in
the secret of the verse "A virtuous woman is a crown to her
husband" (Proverbs 12:4), she then ascends to Binah, which is
the secret of yod hey, and together with herself, which is hey,
gives us the secret of yod hey hey. And these three letters, yod
hey hey, are to be found as a crown on the head of the waw,
which is Ze'ir Anpin. And on the text: "And for this reason,
Keter..." is yod hey hey, three letters, i.e. yod hey that is in
Binah and Malkhut itself, which is hey, become kaph, i.e.
Keter (a crown) over the waw which is Ze'ir Anpin. And this
is the secret of the verse: "A virtuous woman is a crown to her
husband" (Proverbs 12:4).

849) The sixth commandment of Malkhut is the hand
phylactery which is to be placed on the left arm, which is
Gevurah, and from the side of Gevurah it is the hey of weak
hand, which is Malkhut. And therefore the hand phylactery,
which is Malkhut, must be placed on the left arm, which is
Gevurah of Ze'ir Anpin. And from Keter to Gevurah are five
Sephirot [Keter, Hokhmah, Binah, Hesed, Gevurah], and they
are the aspect of the head phylactery of the central column,
which is Ze'ir Anpin. For from Keter to Gevurah is the aspect
of the head phylactery, for they are Ze'ir Anpin, and below
Gevurah they are the hand phylactery, for they are Malkhut.
And she, Malkhut, is the knot of the three straps, namely
Netsach, Hod, and Yesod; i.e. she is the knot of the two straps
of the head, which are Netsach and Hod, and the knot of the
one strap of the hand phylactery, which is Yesod. And it
follows that she is the knot of the three straps.

850) And she is the seventh commandments, which is the
precept of fringes, comprised of blue and white, which are
Judgement and Mercy. In the flame of the candle, the white
fire does not devour what is under it, for it is attached only to
the blue fire that is under it, but the blue fire of the candle is
attached to the wick and the oil, and it devours and destroys
what is under it (as above, Bereshit Beit 249-268), for the
white fire is Hesed and the blue fire is Judgement. And about
the blue fire, which is Judgement, it is said: "Then (the fire)
consumed the burnt-offering" (I Kings 18:38), for the white is
from the right and the blue from the left, while the central
column, which is the unity of the two of them, of the right
side and the left side, is green. For this reason the sages taught:
From what time in the morning may the Shema Israel be
recited? As soon as one can distinguish between blue and white
(Mishnah, Berakhot 1, 2), i.e. as soon as he can distinguish
between Hesed and Judgement, for he has to unite them in the

central column, this being the secret of the recitation of the Shema Israel. And this is why it was decreed that the section about the fringes (Numbers 15:37-41) be included in the unity of the recital of the Shema Israel, because its precept is to be fulfilled with white and blue, which have to be brought together in the recital of the Shema Israel.

851) And she is the eighth commandment, which is mezuzah. The Shekhinah is called mezuzah from the point of view of the central column, i.e. Ze'ir Anpin, which is the letters (of the Tetragrammaton) yod hey waw and hey, and from the point of view of the Righteous One, which is Yesod, which is the secret of the covenant that is called Shadday (Almighty). Shadday is the seal of the king, who is the Tetragrammaton [yod hey waw and hey]. Therefore there is a Tetragrammaton inside the mezuzah, corresponding to the central column, and the word Shadday (Almighty) on the outside of the mezuzah, corresponding to Yesod.

852) The ninth commandment is the Shekhinah, which is called the sign of the covenant from the point of view of the Righteous One, the Foundation of the World, which is Yesod, as it is written: "This is the sign of the covenant" (Genesis 9:17). "This" refers to the Shekhinah and it is "the sign of the covenant." And it is written: "It is a sign between Me and the Children of Israel forever; for in six days the Lord made the heaven and the earth, and on the seventh day He ceased from work and rested" (Exodus 31:17). "Between Me and the Children of Israel," i.e. between the central column, which is Ze'ir Anpin, and Netsach and Hod, termed the Children of Israel. "Sign" refers to the Righteous One, i.e. Yesod. "It is" [hi'] refers to the Shekhinah. "For in six days the Lord made the heaven and the earth," i.e. from Keter to the central column, which is Tipheret, this being the six Sephirot, Keter,

Hokhmah, Binah, Hesed, Gevurah and Tipheret, for whenever six is mentioned it is only from the point of view of the letter waw, which is Tipheret. Here, too, the six days refer to Tipheret, together with the five Sephirot that precede it, and which it includes. But from Tipheret and downwards it is no longer the aspect of Ze'ir Anpin, but rather the aspect of Malkhut. And there is no seventh, other than from the point of view of the letter yod, which is Malkhut, which is a diadem on the head of Ze'ir Anpin in the secret of the verse "A virtuous woman is a diadem to her husband" (Proverbs 12:4). And she is then in the aspect of upper Hokhmah and is called 'ot hu' (It is), in the masculine form. And when Malkhut is lower Hokhmah it is called 'ot hi' (It is), in the feminine form. And this is why the written text (Exodus 31:17) is "'ot hu,'" with a waw, i.e. in the masculine form, although it is pointed with a chireq (vowel "i"), showing how it is to be read in the feminine form: 'ot hi.'

853) And circumcision was decreed for the eighth, namely the eight Sephirot from Hokhmah to Yesod (Hokhmah, Binah, Hesed, Gevurah, Tipheret, Netsach, Hod, and Yesod), to receive in them the small yod which is Malkhut, and to elevate her to Keter, for her to be a diadem over the head of the eight Sephirot. And it was decreed that the foreskin be placed in a vessel with dust (cf. Pirkey d'Rabbi Eliezer, chapter 29), in order to fulfil the verse "And dust shall be serpent's food" (Isaiah 65:25).

854) The tenth commandment that is with Malkhut is: "And the Children of Israel shall keep the Sabbath" (Exodus 31:16). The Shekhinah is called sabbath, from the point of view of the three upper stages, namely shin, [the form of the letter having three arms — tr.] which alludes to the three Sephirot Keter, Hokhmah, and Binah. And Malkhut is daughter and is fourth

to these three. "Six days" (Exodus 31:15) refers to the six Sephirot from Hesed to Yesod, i.e. Hesed, Gevurah, Tipheret, Netsach, Hod, and Yesod, on which work may be done, because the building of the world commences with Hesed, as it is written: "A world is built from Hesed" (Psalms 89:3). [The usual rendering is: "Forever in mercy built" — tr.]. But from Binah and upwards, i.e. in the upper three Sephirot, she is rest and pleasure and cessation from all work.

855) The eleventh commandment that is with Malkhut is called the morning, afternoon, and evening prayers, from the point of view of the three patriarchs, (cf. Talmud Bavli, Berakhot 26b), namely Hesed, Gevurah, and Tipheret. It is the prayer of every [kol] mouth [peh], [sixteenth blessing of the Shemoneh Esreh, Sephardi only], i.e. Malkhut cleaving to Yesod, for prayer is Malkhut and every mouth is Yesod. For the word kol (all or every) only means the Righteous One, which is Yesod, as it is written: "For kol is in the heaven and in the earth" (I Chronicles 29:11), which Yonathan Ben Uziel translated (into Aramaic) as "that takes hold of heaven and earth, i.e. Yesod that is attached to heaven and earth that are Ze'ir Anpin and Malkhut. Mouth [peh: peh hey, 80 + 5 = 85] has the same numerical value as circumcision [milah: mem yod lamed hey, 40 + 10 + 30 + 5 = 85], and just as Male and Female below unite with the covenant, so, too the bride and bridegroom above come together in Yesod, they being Ze'ir Anpin and Malkhut. Yesod is the Life [chay: chet yod, 8 + 10 = 18] of the Worlds, because it includes the 18 blessings of the Amidah prayer (Shemoneh Esreh), as it is written: "Blessings are upon the head of the righteous" (Proverbs 10:6).

856) And for this reason when one bows (during the prayer) one should bow at (the word) 'Blessed,' which is the secret of Yesod, and when returning to the upright position, one should

do so (at the mention of) the Divine Name. (Cf. Talmud Bavli, Berakhot 12a bot.) This is the Shekhinah in the name of the Tetragrammaton, with which the Shekhinah has to be stood upright, the same about whom it is said: "The virgin of Israel is fallen; she shall rise no more" (Amos 5:2) by and within herself, but she shall by another stage, namely, the Tetragrammaton, i.e. Ze'ir Anpin, and for this reason: "In that day I will raise up the [succah] tabernacle of David that is fallen" (ibid 9:11); and the reference is to Him, about whom it is said: "The Tetragrammaton raises up those that are bowed down" (Psalms 146:8), and, therefore, when returning to the upright position, one should do so at the Divine Name.

857) The twelfth commandment that is with Malkhut is called the Festival of Unleavened Bread (Passover) and the Festival of Weeks and the Festival of Succot, from the point of view of the three patriarchs, which are Hesed, Gevurah, and Tipheret; and the New Year is the aspect of Malkhut herself, which is the secret of: The law of the government [Malkhut] is law. (Cf. Talmud Bavli, Gittin 10b.) There is also the opinion that the Festival of Passover is the right arm, i.e. Hesed; the Festival of Weeks, which is the time when the Torah was given in the wilderness, where the appointee over the wilderness is ox from the side of Gevurah — the Festival of Weeks thus is Gevurah; and the Festival of Succot is Tipheret as it is said: "And Jacob journeyed to Succot" (Genesis 33:17), Jacob being Tipheret. And in all other places, the author says that Passover is Hesed, Succot Gevurah, and Weeks is Tipheret. The thirteenth commandment that is with Malkhut is the recital of the Shema Israel.

EXPLANATIONS OF THE HOLY NAMES AND
APPELLATIVES

858) And it should be known that the Infinite One is called
Wise One in all sorts of wisdom, and Understanding One in all
sorts of understanding, and Pious One in all sorts of piety, and
Mighty One in all sorts of might, and Counsellor in all sorts of
counsel, and Righteous One in all sorts of righteousness, and
King in all sorts of kingship, infinitely and immeasurably. And
in all these stages, in one He is called Merciful One and in
another He is called Judge, and so on in a number of stages
until the Infinite One. This poses a question, for it implies that
there is change in Him between Merciful One and Judge, but
this is not so, for before He created the world, He was called
in all these stages after the names of the creatures of the world,
why should He have been called Merciful One, Judge, for there
would have been none for Him to show mercy to. Thus He was
indeed so called after the creatures that were in the future to
be created, but there is not, heaven forbid, any change in Him
Himself.

859) And for this reason, all the Names are appellatives of
Him, because of His deeds. In such a way He created the soul
[neshamah] in His likeness, which is so named following its
actions in each of the parts of the body, which is itself called a
small world. Just as the Master of the Universe behaves with
each creature in each generation according to His deeds, so also
is the soul [neshamah] according to the deeds of each part. That
same part of the body with which he observes a precept is
called soul [neshamah] because of compassion, loving-kindness,
grace and mercy that are active in his body. And that part of
his body with which he commits a transgression is called soul
because of judgement and wrath and anger that are active in
his body. But away from body, for whom can there be
compassion or cruelty because of the deeds of the body?

860) So, too, for whom could the Master of the Universe have been called Merciful One, Gracious One or Judge prior to His creating the world and His creating His creatures? Thus all His names are appellatives, and He is so called only after the creatures of the world. Thus, when the members of the generation are good, i.e. He is for them called the Tetragrammaton [yod hey waw and hey] in the attribute of Mercy. But when the members of the generation are wicked, He is for them called 'The Lord' [aleph dalet nun yod] in the attribute of Justice. For He is called after the quality of each generation and of each person, but He Himself has no specific quality and no specific name.

861) Consider the Sephirot, where each Sephirah has a specific name, quality, border, and limit. The Master of the Universe spreads throughout these names and rules by them and is called after them and is enclothed in them and lives amongst them as a soul [neshamah] within the parts of the body. And just as the Master of the Worlds has no specific name and no specific place, but His rule is in all directions in the world, so also the soul [neshamah] has neither name nor place anywhere in the body, but its rule is in every direction, and there is no part of the body that is free of her.

862) And for this reason, no one place should be noted as that of the soul in the body, for, otherwise, if one place is so noted it would follow that her rule is lacking in the remaining parts of the body. Nor is she to be called by one, two, or even three names, saying that she is Hokhmah or from Binah, that she has Da'at, and no others, for if one does this, it would follow that she lacks the other stages.

863) And this is even truer with respect to the Master of the Universe, to whom no place should be ascribed nor specific

name attributed, nor should He be doubled or tripled in them,
i.e. the stage of the Chariot, in which it is said "They thrice
ascribe holiness to You" [Additional Service, repetition of the
Shemoneh Esreh by the reader, Sephardi text only — tr.], since
all the stages of all His Chariots are tripled, as in "The
Patriarchs are the Heavenly Chariot" (cf. Midrash Bereshit
Rabba 47, 6), namely the likeness of lion, ox, eagle. For they
are a chariot for man, and it is said of them: "As for the
likeness of their faces, they had the face of a man" (Ezekiel
1:10). And from the point of the Female, they — lion, ox, eagle
— rule over man, which is the (generic) name of the Female,
and the Female is a chariot for lion, ox, eagle. And this is why
it is said about her "They thrice ascribe holiness to You."

864) Similarly, the letters yod hey waw, that allude to the
faces of the celestial beings, lion, ox, and eagle, are tripled,
thus: yod hey waw; hey waw yod; and waw hey yod. Hey is a
fourth for them and is the secret of "They thrice ascribe
holiness to You," as above. She is the peace-offerings [root:
shin lamed mem] of all of them, for in all of them she
completes [root: shin lamed mem] the Name of the
Tetragrammaton. But neither names nor letters must be tripled
for the Master of All, for He is called by all the names and has
no one specific Name, and every single name testifies about
Him that He is Master of All the Worlds, and the name 'The
Lord' [aleph dalet nun yod] testifies about Him.

865) And there is a person who inherits three hundred and ten
worlds, as it is written: "That I may cause those that love Me to
inherit substance [yesh: yod shin, 10 + 300 = 310]" (Proverbs
8:21) (Mishnah, Uktzin 3, 12). This is according to the level of
Hokhmah that is called something from nothing, for Keter is
called nihility and Hokhmah, substance, is drawn *ex nihilo*, and
this is upper Hokhmah. And there is also the person who only

inherits one world, according to his level as has been taught: Every righteous man has a world for himself (Midrash Exodus Rabba 52, 3). Likewise every person in Israel [i.e. every member of the Jewish people — tr.] inherits a world according to his level on high, but there is no recording of a world for the Master of the Universe, for He is the Master of All the Worlds, and the name 'The Lord' [aleph dalet nun yod] testifies about Him.

866) Likewise with the Name of the Tetragrammaton, on which all beings depend, and all His celestial beings testify about the Master of the Universe that He pre-existed all beings, that He is within all beings, and that He will be after all beings. And this is the secret that the celestial beings testify about Him, that He was, is, and will be.

867) Dina [dalet yod nun aleph, the Aramaic word for law] is composed of the letters of The Lord' [aleph dalet nun yod], re-arranged. And for this reason, our teachers of blessed memory said: The law of the government is law (cf. Talmud Bavli, Gittin 10b). The name 'el (God or power) testifies about the Master of All that no name, being, stage, and certainly none of the other creatures has any ability apart from Him. And this is as is written: "And all the inhabitants of the earth are reputed as nothing; and He does according to His will in the host of heaven, and among the inhabitants of the earth" (Daniel 4:32). Elohim [aleph lamed hey yod mem, God] testifies to His Divinity, that He is the God, and the God of Gods, and He is God over All, and there in no God beside Him. Ts'va'ot (Hosts) testifies about Him, as it is written: "He does according to His will in the host of heaven" (Daniel 4:32). Shadday [Almighty, shin dalet yod] testifies about Him that [she, shin], when He said to the world "Enough" [day: dalet yod], the world stopped and did not expand any more. Likewise, to the water, spirit, and fire He said: "Enough" [day].

868) Likewise, every being and every name testifies about Him, for when He was alone, before He created the world, why did He need to be called by these names or by the other appellatives, such as Merciful One, Gracious one, Long-suffering, Judge, Mighty, Strong? There are many such names that are so coined after all the worlds and the creatures in them in order to show that His rule is over them.

869) And it is likewise with the soul [neshamah], which, in the aspect of its rule over all the parts of the body, is likened to Him. Just as He is ruler over all the words, so is the soul ruler over all parts of the body, but the soul is not like Him in its essence, for it was He who created it, while there is no God above Him who created Him. Furthermore there are a number of changes and incidents and causes that happen to the soul, which is not the case for the Master of All. For this reason, the soul is like Him only respecting its rule over all parts of the body, but not in any other respect.

THE RECITAL OF THE SHEMA ISRAEL AND PHYLACTERIES

870) Futhermore, the word 'Hear' [Shema: shin mem ayyin] in the Shema Israel consists of the letters of shem [shin mem, name] and the letter ayyin, which is written especially large. Similarly, the letter dalet of one [echad: aleph chet dalet] is written large, and these two large letters spell 'ed [ayin dalet, witness]. Thus, between the shin mem of shema [shin mem ayyin], which is Malkhut that is called name [shem: shin mem], and the aleph chet of one [echad: aleph chet dalet], which is Ze'ir Anpin, are to be found the large letters ayyin dalet, which are the secret of the verse: "The Lord is witness against you" (I Samuel 12:5). And He is indeed a witness over everyone

who proclaims His unity in the world. And therefore David said: "As for me, I will rejoice [esmach: aleph sin mem chet]" and the aleph chet of echad [aleph chet dalet] together with the shin mem of Shema, spell 'I will rejoice' [esmach: aleph sin mem chet]. And this is the secret of the unity of Ze'ir Anpin and Malkhut, from the aspect of being manifest, for Malkhut, from the aspect of being manifest is called name [shem: shin mem].

871) Futhermore, the large letter dalet (whose numerical value is 4) of one [echad: aleph chet dalet] alludes to the four compartments of the phylacteries that aleph chet of One [echad: aleph chet dalet], which is Ze'ir Anpin, lays, and with which He is adorned, and they are an ornament on His head. And they are the secret of the combination yod hey hey waw. The yod, which is Hokhmah, is diadem on hey which is the daughter, i.e. Malkhut. Thus, "The Lord by wisdom [Hokhmah] founded the earth" (Proverbs 3:19), for Father, which is the secret of Hokhmah, founded the daughter, which is Malkhut, that is called earth. The second hey of the combination yod hey hey waw is upper Mother, which is a diadem on the waw, which is the son, i.e. Ze'ir Anpin, as we read: "By understanding He established the heaven (ibid), for Ze'ir Anpin, who is called heavens, receives the intelligences from Understanding, i.e. upper Mother, for Mother established the son. Thus, in the world-to-come, which is Binah, there is no eating and no drinking, but the righteous sit with their crowns on their heads. (Cf. Talmud Bavli, Berakhot 17a.) The righteous here are Ze'ir Anpin, who has a crown on His head, from Binah that is called the next world.

TWO ARRANGEMENTS OF THE FOUR SECTIONS OF
THE PHYLACTERIES

872) And the daughter, which is Malkhut, is the phylactery of the weak hand. Yod is its knot. Upper hey, i.e. Mother, is the head phylactery on the head of Tipheret. His phylacteries, i.e. His intelligences, are according to the arrangement yod hey waw hey, where "Sanctify unto Me" (Exodus 13:1-10) is yod. "And it shall be when the Lord shall bring you into the Land" (Exodus 13:11-16) is hey; "Hear, O Israel" (the Shema Israel, Deuteronomy 6:4-9) is waw; and "And it shall come to pass if you will hearken diligently" (Deuteronomy 11:13-21) is the final hey. This arrangement is for the head phylactery of Ze'ir Anpin. But in the next world, which is Binah, the phylacteries, namely, the intelligences that she receives, have the order with the beings, which are hey hey, in the center. That is, Yod, which is "Sanctify unto Me;" the waw (Shema) last; "And it shall be when the Lord shall bring you into the Land" and "And it shall come to pass if you hearken diligently," that is hey-hey, are in the middle. And on this the prophet said: "But let him that glories glory in this that he understands and knows Me, that I am the Lord" (Jeremiah 9:23) [where the initial letters of the second, third, fourth, and fifth Hebrew words spell yod hey hey waw] (and see in the Introduction to the Tikkunei ha-Zohar, page 95b). And this is why the sages of the Mishnah taught: There is room on the head to lay two pairs of phylacteries (cf. Talmud Bavli, Eruvin, 95b). And such a one is privileged to observe two precepts, about which they taught: Not everyone has the privilege to enjoy two tables (cf. Talmud Bavli, Berakhot 5b).

873) In the four sections of the head phylacteries, the yod, which is the section "Sanctify unto Me" (Exodus 13:1-10), is Hokhmah. The hey, which is the section "And it shall be when the Lord shall bring you into the land" (Exodus 13:11-16), is

Binah. Waw, which is the section "Hear, O Israel"
(Deuteronomy 6:4-9), is the central column. And the hey,
which is the section "And it will come to pass if you will
diligently hearken" (Deuteronomy 11:13-21), is holy Malkhut.
The head that is crowned with these four sections of Keter,
which is the circumference of the head that comprises the
phylacteries that are the intelligences and covers them. The
recital of the Shema Israel is love, Hesed, and is equivalent to
the Torah that was given on the right. The phylacteries, called
oz, strength, are on the left side, which is Gevurah. The central
column, which is Tipheret, includes everything, for it
comprises Hesed and Gevurah. The wings of the precept, which
are the fringes in which are blue and white, are Netsach and
Hod. The mezuzah, on which is recorded the Name Shadday
(Almighty), is Righteous One, i.e. Yesod, and the Shekhinah is
the gate onto which the mezuzah is affixed, about which it is
written: "This is the gate of the Lord" (Psalms 118:20).

874) Furthermore, the three-headed letter shin is the three
straps, the two of the head phylactery and the one of the arm
phylactery. Dalet is the knot of the head phylactery at the back
of the head, while yod is the knot of the hand phylactery.
Together [shin, dalet, and yod] they spell Shadday (Almighty).
This is why Shadday is written on the outside of the
phylacteries, while the Tetragrammaton is inside the
phylacteries, for it is the four sections therein. The
four-headed letter shin alludes to the four compartments of the
phylacteries. Shadday [shin dalet yod, $300 + 4 + 10 = 314$] is
His, Ze'ir Anpin's, sign, and has the same numerical value as
Metatron [mem tet tet resh waw nun, $40 + 9 + 9 + 200 + 6 + 50 = 314$].

875) Again: yod, Hokhmah, is the section "Sanctify unto Me"
(Exodus 13:1-10). Hey, Binah, is the section "And it shall be

when the Lord bring you into the land" (Exodus 13:11-16).
Waw is the Shema Israel, in which there are six words: "Hear,
O-Israel, the-Lord our-God, the-Lord is-One" (Deuteronomy
6:4), alluding to the six Sephirot which are six branches of the
tree which Tipheret includes. The last hey (of the
Tetragrammaton) is the section "And it will come to pass if you
will hearken diligently" (Deuteronomy 11:13-21) which is
Malkhut. These are the intelligences of the head, for the head,
which is Keter, is the secret of the letter kaph, in the secret of
the verse: "There is none holy as [kaph] the Lord, for there is
none beside You" (1 Samuel 2:2), where the letter kaph (as) in
the expression "as the Lord" is Keter of Ze'ir Anpin.

876) Shadday (Almighty) alludes to the straps, compartments,
and knots of the phylacteries from the outside, for the shin of
Shadday [shin dalet yod], with its three-heads, alludes to the
three straps, two of the head and one of the hand. The dalet of
Shadday [shin dalet yod], having the numerical value of 4,
alludes to the four compartments of the head phylactery, and
also to the knot of dalet that is behind the head. The yod of
Shadday [shin, dalet, yod] alludes to the knot of the hand
phylactery. The same holds for the mezuzah, there being a
Tetragrammaton on the inside and the name Shadday on the
outside. The four-headed letter shin, with the dalet (numerical
value of 4), of Shadday alludes to the four compartments and
to the knot of the head phylactery behind the head, which has
the shape of a double dalet. Likewise, there is a double shin,
one on the right side of the compartment and one on the left
side of the compartment. The yod of Shadday [shin dalet yod]
is the knot of the phylactery of the weak hand, which is the
fifth compartment: that is to say that with the four
compartments of the head phylactery the fifth compartment is
that of the hand phylactery. The dalet of Shadday [shin dalet
yod] is the brain, about which it has been taught; the place on

the head where a child's brain is seen to pulsate (cf. Talmud Bavli, Menachot 37a), and this is a child suckling from the breasts [shin dalet yod] of its mother, i.e. from Shadday [Almighty, shin dalet yod], for the dalet alludes to the intelligences of the upper three Sephirot of suckling.

877) The phylacteries of the Master of the Universe are Keter. And what is Keter of the Master of the Universe? It is the Tetragrammaton [yod, hey, waw and hey]; namely, the yod of the Tetragrammaton is Hokhmah, hey is Binah, and waw is Tipheret, which includes the six Sephirot Hesed, Gevurah, and Tipheret, Netsach, Hod and Yesod. The final hey (of the Tetragrammaton) is Malkhut, i.e. ten Sephirot. And this is the reason behind the verses "Who is like [kaph] Your people, like [kaph] Israel, one people on earth" (II Samuel 7:23); "For [kaph yod] what great nation is there, that has God so near to them, as [kaph] the Lord our God is whenever we call upon Him?" (Deuteronomy 4:7); and also the verse, mentioned above: "There is none holy as [kaph] the Lord, for there is none beside You" (I Samuel 2:2) (772). These four verses all have in them the letter kaph, and the secret of the letter kaph (whose numerical value is 20) is yod yod (the numerical value of each being 10), namely the yod at the beginning and the yod at the end of the combination yod aleph hey dalet waw nun hey yod (which is composed of the letters of the Tetragrammaton, yod hey waw and hey, interwoven with the letters of 'The Lord,' aleph dalet nun yod). And this is the inner meaning of the verse "weighing ten shekels apiece, after the shekel of the sanctuary" (Numbers 7:86) (the literal rendering of which is: ten ten apiece [kaph] in the shekel of the sanctuary), i.e. the kaph of Keter [kaph tav resh], that is composed of ten Sephirot, as above, and they comprise ten Sephirot of direct light, from above downwards, and ten Sephirot of reflected light, which are upwards from below.

878) And these twenty Sephirot, of direct light and of reflected light, are the secret of the verse "And the waters that are above the heavens" (Psalms 148:4), which are the male upper waters, i.e. the ten Sephirot of direct light, while "the waters which are under the firmament" (Genesis 1:7) are the female lower waters, i..e the ten Sephirot of reflected light. And Rabbi Akiva said to his pupils about them: When you reach the stones of pure marble, do not say: Water, water (cf. Talmud Bavli, Hagigah, 14b), lest you endanger your souls, for it is not water as is usually understood, i.e. hasadim, but flowing light; i.e. it is also composed of Hokhmah that is called light, and from the aspect of hasadim, it is flowing. This is why it was likened to flowing water. And this light is never interrupted, nor is it cut off, nor separated (and see above, 868). And because it is from Keter, it is called water without end, for Keter is called the Infinite One (literally: The Unending One).

THE FESTIVAL OF WEEKS

879) "You shall present a burnt-offering for a sweet savor unto the Lord" (Numbers 28:27). Come and see: About Passover it is written: "You shall present an offering made by fire, a burnt- offering unto the Lord" (ibid. v.19). About the Festival of Weeks it is not written "an offering made by fire," but "You shall present a burnt-offering" (ibid.). What is the reason for this? The reason is that this day, of the Festival of Weeks, is that on which the bride enters the wedding canopy; i.e. Malkhut enters the wedding canopy with Ze'ir Anpin, and Israel comes from the period of the counting of the days and weeks of purity, and is taken in and enters into these days of purity, namely, the secret of the seven days Hesed, Gevurah, Tipheret, Netsach, Hod, Yesod, and Malkhut, in each one of

which are Hesed, Gevurah, Tipheret, Netsach, Hod, Yesod, and Malkhut, making a total of 49 (7 x 7) days. And she, Malkhut, has emerged from everything bad, i.e. there is no more any hold over her, and has observed the days of purity as fitting, i.e. the 49 days of the counting [of the Omer, between Passover and the Festival of Weeks — tr.], and this is the secret of the king who tasted the taste of a virgin (cf. Talmud Bavli, Megilah 13a). In other words, the secret of the verse "A virgin, neither had any man known her" (Genesis 24:16), if the matter be disclosed, is that no one of the evil forces had any hold over her. And this is why it is not written about it (the Festival of Weeks) "an offering made by fire," for no other came close to the Sanctuary, which is Malkhut, and the other party has already removed from there. Thus there are not, nor is there any need for, offerings made by fire in this case, for Israel has removed themselves from the evil side. Said Rabbi Abba: We still have to open this matter up.

COMMENTARY:

The offerings made by fire are judgments (as above, in the Commentator's Interpolation, par. 6 & 7, q.v.) and since here (at the Festival of Weeks), Malkhut has already emerged from all the judgments that were with her, it is therefore not written You shall present an offering made by fire, a burnt-offering, but "You shall present a burnt-offering" (Numbers 28:27).

880) Rabbi Shimeon said: I lifted up my hands in prayer to Him who created the world and found this secret in the works

of the early masters: Offerings made by fire are in between the good and the bad, and they come on this side and on that side, for they are attached to the Tree of Knowledge of Good and Evil, and are, therefore, attached to both the good and to the bad. For this reason, on the other days, it is written: "an offering made by fire, a burnt-offering," for they contain judgments and have a hold on the Tree of Knowledge of Good and Evil. But on these days when the Tree of Life and no other is to be found, i.e. on the Festival of Weeks, we do not need an offering made by fire, and it does not have to be there, for this day of the Festival of Weeks belongs to the Tree of Life and not the Tree of Knowledge of Good and Evil. This is why Scripture says: "You shall present a burnt-offering for a sweet savor unto the Lord" (Numbers 28:27), and not an offering made by fire, a burnt-offering to the Lord. And the meaning of 'burnt-offering' [olah] is from the word to ascend, for it ascends [olah] to the Most High One, as we have learned. And we have already clarified these matters in the commentary about one-year old bullocks and the whole of that offering.

ROSH HA-SHANAH (THE NEW YEAR)

881) "And in the seventh month, on the first day of the month" (Numbers 29:1). This is as we have learned, that the day of the New Year is the Day of Judgement for the whole world: stringent judgement on the first day and lenient judgement on the second day. [The New Year, although technically one day, is kept for two. — tr.]. There is a question to be asked here: It is written: "And you shall make a burnt-offering" (ibid. v.2), whereas it should have been written: And you shall present a burnt-offering, as on all the other days. What is the special meaning of "And you shall make?" The answer to this is that on this day of the New Year

it is written: "And make me savory food" (Genesis 27:4), which is what Isaac said to Esau, who is the accuser. And during these days Israel makes many savory foods and dishes, i.e. precepts and prayers, while the accuser goes to search for the sins of the world, to make them into foods for the prosecution. It is therefore not written: And you shall present a burnt-offering, but: "And you shall make a burnt-offering" (Numbers 29:2), i.e. make and correct savory foods. And it is not written: An offering made by fire, a burnt-offering, as it is for all the other festival days, for during these days there is no part for the evil forces. Nor is "an offering made by fire" written for the Festival of Weeks and the Day of Atonement, and certainly not for this day (the New Year), on which we made savory foods and dishes without knowledge of the evil forces, for he (the evil forces, Esau) had been sent by Isaac to hunt game (cf. Genesis 27:3), i.e. the iniquities of mortal men, and to bring them to him.

COMMENTARY:

Part of all the sacrifices is given to the evil forces (as above, in the Commentator's Interpolation, par. 2-13, q.v.), but on this day of the New Year it is the reverse, for, with the sounding of the shophar, Satan's mind is confused. This means that the sounding of the shophar has the effect of annulling the upper three Sephirot of the left, which is where the life force of the evil forces come from. Because on the New Year, the first state of Malkhut is in control and this is the secret of what Isaac, who is the left-hand column, said to Esau: "And hunt game for me" (Genesis 27:3), for he gave him permission to draw down the upper three Sephirot of the left, and to awaken all the judgments that come with him, this being the secret of "And Isaac trembled very exceedingly" (ibid. v.33). And these judgments begin to awaken on the New Year, but meanwhile, Israel takes advice from Rebecca: take a shophar and sound it, as is explained below in the next paragraph. That is, the sounding of the shophar causes a contraction of the upper three Sephirot of the left, which are all the intelligences of the evil forces, and they, the evil forces, are thereby confused. It follows that they, the evil forces, not only do not have any part of the sacrifices of the New Year, as they do with the other sacrifices, but they lose all their grip and become confused (and see above, Emor, 187-224).

And on the text: "And certainly not for this day (the New Year), on which we make savory foods and dishes without knowledge of the evil forces;" i.e. Not only is he not given any life forces from the sacrifices, but his mind is also confused. "For he (the evil forces, Esau) had been sent by Isaac to hunt game... i.e. the iniquities of mortal men." Because he is in the first state of Malkhut, for Isaac, who is the secret of the left hand column, sits on the Throne of Judgement, and wishes to increase his rule, and therefore sends Esau out to hunt game — that is that he should draw down the upper three Sephirot of the left. And since he gave his permission, the judgments immediately awaken, and they find the whole world guilty. And, as explained in the following paragraph, while he is yet on the way, i.e. before he has managed to reveal the judgments from the upper three Sephirot of the left side, they take a shophar and sound it in order to awaken Mercy, for the sounding of the shophar causes the upper three Sephirot of the left side to be cancelled, and the evil forces can no longer draw them down and their mind becomes confused, and in their stead are drawn down the savory dishes of Jacob, which are mercies.

882) And while he is yet on the way, Israel takes advice from Rebecca: keep all these rituals and all the prayers, and take a shophar and sound it in order to awaken Mercy, as has been explained in the preceding paragraph. And we have already learnt: "And he brought him wine and he drank" (Genesis 27:25), for he came from far, from Binah, from that place where the wine is old, which is the secret of the illumination of Hokhmah of the six intermediate Sephirot of the left side, after the annulment of the upper three Sephirot of the left side, this being termed old wine. And he drank, found it tasty, and rejoiced. And after that Isaac, who is the left column, blessed him with a number of blessings and removed his iniquities, for the illumination of Hokhmah makes atonement for iniquities. As it is written: "And Jacob was yet scarce gone out from the presence of Isaac his father, and Esau his brother came in from his hunting" (Genesis 27:30), i.e. he was carrying with him a number of burdens of iniquities, as has been stated, and we have already learned these matters (above, Emor, 218-219).

883) And this is why it is a day of the sounding of the shophar, and the sacrifice is a burnt-offering. "One ram... one he-goat for a sin-offering" (Numbers 29:8 & 11). "One ram [ayil]" — this is, as we have learned, because of the ram of Isaac. The "one he-goat for a sin-offering" is a bribe to Samael, for from just this offering he receives some nourishment from the aspect of the six intermediate Sephirot of Hokhmah, to make atonement before him for having wept on that day when he realized that he had not done his will and had gone hunting for nothing (see Genesis 27:34). For the upper three Sephirot of his left side had been annulled, and they are his total strength, as above, and the contraction of the upper three Sephirot is called weeping, as we have learned. And on the Day of Atonement the story is similar, and it is written out in Parashat Emor (227-257).

THE FESTIVAL OF TABERNACLES (SUCCOT)

884) "And on the fifteenth day of the seventh month" (Numbers 29:12). Rabbi Abba began by quoting: "And the ark rested in the seventh month" (Genesis 8:4). Come and see: Throughout all these days, from the Day of Atonement to the Festival of Succot, the Mother, which is the Shekhinah, goes over the sons, who are Israel, so that the evil forces should not have control over Israel, and in order to save them. After the children have been saved and are sitting in their booths [succot], they are guarded with the protection of Mother, which is the Shekhinah. On the first and second days of the Festival of Succot, she commanded Israel to make a feast for the ministering angels of the other nations, namely the seventy bullocks for the seventy ministers, and she does not rest there with them. On the third day (of the festival), which is the seventeenth day of the month, the Shekhinah begins to rest on them. And this is the meaning of the verse: "And the ark rested in the seventh month, on the seventeenth day of the month, upon the mountains of Ararat" (Genesis 8:4), where the ark is the secret of the Shekhinah, and the mountains of Ararat are the mountains in the midst of which rest all the curses and all the punishments, for they are the appointees of the nations.

885) Rabbi Elazar said: On the first day of the Festival, Malkhut does not rest on them, on the ministers of the seventy nations, nor on the second day; but only on the third day, which spoils by the addition, does she rest on them, adding letters and spoiling sacrifices, as it is written: "Eleven [ashtey asar] bullocks" (Numbers 29:20), which is appropriate for the evil eye. For on the first day and the second day there is rejoicing for the sons, and Israel distributes to them, to the appointees of the nations, booty. From the third day and onwards, when the Shekhinah rests upon them, what is written?

"And the water decreased continually until the tenth month; in the tenth month, on the first day of the month, were the tops of the mountains seen" (Genesis 8:5). "And the waters decreased continually;" these are the sacrifices that are continually reduced, and as they become fewer in number so does their goodness become less.

COMMENTARY:

Malkhut is built up mainly from the left column, which is the illumination of Hokhmah of the left side. However, when she rests on Israel, she is mating with Ze'ir Anpin, which is the secret of the central column, for the Hokhmah that is in Malkhut then illuminates only from below upwards. And its main illumination is in the aspect of the hasadim that it receives from Ze'ir Anpin. But when Malkhut rests on the nations of the world and the evil forces, it is the opposite, for she rests on them only when she is separated from Ze'ir Anpin, for the nations and the evil forces have no desire to receive from the central column, which is Ze'ir Anpin, but rather from the aspect of the left that is in Malkhut solely.

And on the text: "Throughout all these days... Mother... goes over the sons, etc." i.e. Malkhut, when she is in a mating with Ze'ir Anpin, which is the central column. "So that the evil forces should not have control over Israel;" i.e. so that the evil forces should not awaken them to draw Hokhmah down from above, from Malkhut, as is the way of the evil forces. "After the children have been saved and are sitting in their booths [succot], they are guarded, etc." Since they have merited the succah, they are guarded with an upper protection, such that the evil forces can no longer have control over them, to incite them into drawing the left side down, from above downwards. Therefore, "she commanded Israel to make a feast for the angels of the other nations;" i.e. that they should sacrifice seventy bullocks, this being the secret of the drawing down of the illumination of the left side to the ministers of the nations and to the evil forces, just to the extent that they should be able to live and subsist only, for the nations and the evil forces have no life and no existence other than from the illumination of the left. "And she does not rest there." For Malkhut does not rest on them unless she is separated from Ze'ir Anpin, for she then increases the life force of the evil forces. Consequently, in order not to give them additional life force, she does not rest on them. But Israel alone draws down for them their portion from the sacrifices, and Israel only draws down illumination, from below upwards, which is according to the correction of the central column. For this illumination comes by way of the three columns, which illuminate towards Malkhut, which is the secret of Hesed and Gevurah, Tipheret, and Malkhut, and after they become included in each other, there are three columns in each one of Hesed and Gevurah, Tipheret, and Malkhut, making 12 altogether, which is the secret of the twelve bullocks (that are offered on the second day of the Festival of Succot, Numbers 29:17), which, inclusively, make thirteen bullocks (that are offered on the first day of the Festival, Numbers 29:13). And the twelve and thirteen bullocks offered respectively on the second and first days of the Festival were in the aspect of the drawing down of Hokhmah in the secret of the three columns and Malkhut that receives them, for when they are included in each other they are the secret of twelve, but, inclusively, they are the secret of thirteen. And on the text: "For on the first day and on the second day there is rejoicing for the sons," and they distribute booty to them: For Israel are the ones who distribute the illumination of the left

side to the appointees of the nations, and they therefore
distribute to them in the secret of the thirteen bullocks on the
first day and the twelve bullocks on the second day. And this is
the secret of the inclusion of the three columns and Malkhut in
each other, as is the way of the illumination of the central
column.

And on the text: "From the third day and onwards, when the
Shekhinah rests upon them, etc." For after they have received
from Israel everything that they are able to illuminate for
them, which is the secret of the twelve bullocks, Malkhut then
begins to rest on the angels of the nations; that is to say, by
virtue of the power of the illumination that they received from
the twelve bullocks that were in holiness, which came from the
central column, they grew stronger and drew down from
Malkhut alone, i.e. in the aspect of herself, which is the left
side without the right side, in order that they should be able to
draw from above downwards as they wish. And this is the
secret of why Israel were then commanded to offer "eleven
[ashtey asar] bullocks" (Numbers 29:20). And on the text: "But
only on the third day, which spoils by the addition, does it rest
on them, adding letters and spoiling sacrifices, as it is written:
'Eleven [ashtey asar] bullocks.'" For on the first and second
days (of the Festival) Israel emanated to them from holiness in
the secret of "Twelve [shtey asar] bullocks" (Numbers 29:17),
which are the secret of the inclusion of the three columns in
each other, as above. But when they (the nations) grew strong
enough to draw down from the aspect of the left side without
the right side, i.e. from Malkhut when in separation, they then
added an evil letter ayin onto the illumination of the twelve
[shtey asar: shin tav yod ayyin sin resh] bullocks that they had
received on the first and second days, and it became eleven
[ashtey asar: ayin shin tav yod ayin sin resh], for when the
letter ayyin is added to twelve [shtey asar], it becomes eleven

[ashtey asar]. It thus follows that they added letters, that is the ayin, and spoilt, reduced the number of the sacrifices, for they no longer have twelve bullocks but only eleven. And so they were continually reduced until they ceased altogether. And on the text: "What is written? 'And the waters decreased continually...'" (Genesis 8:5), these are the sacrifices that are continually reduced, etc.

THE WATER LIBATION

886) Rabbi Shimeon said: Elazar, come and see: From the second day the waters began to appear, i.e. that the libation of water on the altar began (for its purpose was also to draw down life forces and subsistence for the evil forces [as is clarified below, 890: And if he were thirsty, he could pour out water]) — this water is the water that is mentioned here for libation on the days of the Festival. And after the water had begun, and the evil forces and the seventy nations had received the emanation, they then grew in strength, as noted in the preceding paragraph, and from the third day Malkhut rested on them, for they drew her down separated from Ze'ir Anpin, as above. And the Babylonians did not know why these waters are mentioned here in connection with the festival, that is to say that they did not know that their purpose was to provide subsistence to the nations of the world, for the goodness of Israel is not in the place of contraction, i.e. in the fruits of the festival that are reduced in number, but in the place of expansion, and because these waters that are mentioned here are contracting, together with the fruits of the festival, Scripture comes to inform us that it is written: "And the waters decreased continually" (Genesis 8:5). That is, the waters that are known from the days of the festival are the ones that are

mentioned amongst the sacrifices. For on the second day it is said that amongst the sacrifices is "and their drink-offerings" [Veniskeyhem: waw nun samekh kaph yod hey mem] (Numbers 29:18), the last letter of which is mem. And on the sixth day, amongst the offerings is "and the drink-offerings thereof" [unsakheyha: waw nun samekh kaph yod hey] (ibid. v.31), the penultimate letter of which is yod. And on the seventh day "after the ordinance" [kemishpatam: kaph mem shin peh tet mem] (ibid. v.33), the last letter of which is mem. And these three letters together spell waters [mayyim: mem yod mem], from which it follows that there is an allusion to the water libation in the Torah (as is explained in Talmud Bavli, Tannit 2b). For they, the sacrifices, are mountains of curses that continually decrease (as above, 884), and their good, and the emanation that is drawn down on them "decreased continually" (Genesis 8:5). And because these waters belong to them, to the nations and to the evil forces, the letters mem yod mem (spelling mayim, waters) were not joined together and the word did not appear explicitly written in the Torah. But the letters are there, although scattered, with the (first) mem being in "and their drink-offerings" [Veniskeyhem: waw nun samekh kaph yod hey mem, Numbers 29:18], the yod in "and the drink-offerings thereof" [unsakheyha: waw nun samekh kaph yod hey, ibid. v.31], and the final mem in "after their ordinance" [kemishpatam: kaph mem shin peh tet mem, ibid. v.33], as above. And the purpose of this is so that their good should not be all together, but little by little.

887) But regarding Israel, who are from the Holy One, blessed be He, who is the central column, what is written? "But they that seek the Lord will lack no good thing" (Psalms 34:11). The first half of this verse is: "The young lions do lack and suffer hunger" (ibid.). The young lions are the appointees of the other nations. They that seek the Lord are Israel, who will lack no

good thing because they continually ascend higher and higher, for a person may be promoted to a higher degree of sanctity but not demoted [quoted frequently in the Talmud Bavli — tr.]. For this reason, their good, that of the nations and of the evil forces, which are waters, "decreased continually until the tenth month" (Genesis 8:5), which is the month of Tevet, for then are the days of wickedness, for the months of Tevet and Shevat are the period of Judgement and are called the days of wickedness (as is explained in Zohar Chadash, Yitro, 36, q.v.). And this wickedness awakens and grows stronger, and the holy bride, which is Malkhut, is unable to illuminate from the midst of the sun, i.e. is separated from the sun, which is Ze'ir Anpin. And then the tops of these mountains became visible (cf. Genesis 8:5), that is the judgments of the left side that are drawn down with the fruits of the festival, namely, those mountains of darkness and mountains of curses that appear and grow stronger and do evil things in the world.

888) About these days of the Festival of Succot it is written: "And you shall present a burnt-offering, and offering made by fire" (Numbers 29:13). For then these offerings made by fire, which are the judgments (as above, 879), devour their portions, namely, those seventy bullocks corresponding to the seventy angels who rule over the seventy nations. And their number is greatest (namely, thirteen, see v.13) on the first day and decreases with each passing day. And they are called goring bullocks on their days. Rams. [The text here is missing, but should read as follows: "Two rams, fourteen he-lambs of the first year" (Numbers 29:13.)] The two rams on each day [of the seven days of the Festival — tr.] are yod dalet (10 + 4 = 14, the hand of) the Tetragrammaton, for 7 x 2 = 14. And this refers to the hand that controls them continually, every day. And the total number of the he-lambs of the first year is 98, for 7 (days) x 14 (on each day) = 98.

889) And you might wish to ask: If so, if we offer (a total of)
14 rams (during the festival) so that the hand [yad: yod dalet,
10 + 4 = 14] of the Lord will rule; and if we offer 98
he-lambs, which is a bad omen, for it corresponds to the 98
curses in the Admonition — and also it is said that "An arrow
[chets: chet tsade, 8 + 90 = 98) will strike through his liver"
(Proverbs 7:23) — then are we not being evil- minded towards
them, for he says to him: Eat and drink, but his heart is not
with him (cf. Proverbs 23:7)? The answer to this is: Yes, for it
is written: "If your enemy be hungry, give him bread to eat,
and if he be thirsty, give him water to drink; for you will heap
coals of fire upon his head, and the Lord will reward you"
(Proverbs 25:31). But we give only out of rejoicing, for
throughout the whole year, there is no rejoicing like that on
the days of the Festival of Tabernacles [succot], and because we
give out of the goodness of our hearts, in rejoicing and
willingly, our gifts to them turn into coals of fire on their
head, burning coals, for our rejoicing is far from pleasing to
them, i.e. the fourteen rams, seventy bullocks, and 98
he-lambs, which is the sum total of sacrifices, where the
fourteen [14 = 10 + 4, yod dalet: yad, hand] teaches about the
hand of the Tetragrammaton that controls them, and the
seventy bullocks in their decreasing progression teach that their
goodness will continually decrease, while the 98 he-lambs teach
about the 98 curses that rest on them; or in other words: "An
arrow [chets: chet tsade, 8 + 90 = 98] will strike through their
liver" (cf. Proverbs 7:23).

890) And all this is very well, but you might ask: Who asked
us to sacrifice for them, for the appointees of the seventy
nations? Perhaps they are not interested in our doing so? But
all of these appointees have no such rejoicing as that which
they have with all these bullocks and rams and he-lambs that
Israel offers to them at these banquets. Nevertheless, nothing is

offered except to the Holy One, blessed be He, while they, the appointees, come close and the Holy One, blessed be He, distributes to them. And about this it is written: "If your enemy be hungry, give him bread to eat" (Proverbs 25:31), where bread refers to the festival offerings; and in "and if he be thirsty, give him water to drink" (ibid.), water refers to that water that is to be poured out in a libation on the days of the festival, on the second, sixth, and seventh days. And the mnemonic for this is the verse: "Many waters cannot quench the love, neither can the floods drown it; if a man would give all the substances of his house for love, he would utterly be contemned [boz: beit waw zayyin]" (Song of Songs, 8:7), where the numerical values of the letters beit, waw, and zayyin are 2, 6 and 7, respectively.

891) "Many waters cannot quench the love" (Song of Songs 8:7) — this refers to the waters that Israel pours out in libation out of rejoicing and love for the Holy One, blessed be He, as it is written: "Therefore with joy shall you draw water" (Isaiah 12:3). "Neither can the floods drown it" (Song of Songs 8:7). These are the floods of the pure Apharsemon, i.e. the 18 [chay, life] rivers of the emanation that are drawn down from Yesod of Binah (as above, Shemot, 257). For all of them cleave to, and form a bond with, this love. "If a man would give all the substance of his house" (ibid.): this refers to Samael; and he gives "for love" (ibid.) of Israel, i.e. that he should have a portion with them in these waters about which it is written in this section: "If a man would give all the substance of his house for love, he would be utterly contemned", where the root of the word 'contemned,' namely, boz: beit waw zayyin, is a mnemonic for these waters that are poured out on the second, sixth, and seventh days, and the numerical value of beit is 2, of waw is 6, and of zayyin is 7. He would certainly be contemned, for all the substance of Samael is considered for us as a broken potsherd that can never be repaired.

892) And this is explained: The water of Samael, the evil
forces and the nations, is distributed on the days boz [beit waw
zayyin] [i.e. the second, sixth, and seventh days of the festival
— tr.]. This leaves the other days, namely, the third, fourth,
and fifth days of the festival, on which there is no water
libation. The mnemonic for this: He ploughed [charash: chet
resh shin] the furrows of the land, where the letters of charash
stand for chamishi (fifth), revi'i (fourth) and shlishi (third), on
which days there is no libation of water, and they have no
correction through us, nor indeed forever. For just as they have
no correction on the fifth, fourth, and third [charash] days, so
they never have any correction. And should you wish to raise
the point that it is written "He would be utterly contemned"
[literally: Contemned, they contemn him] (Song of Songs 8:7),
whereas, according to the above, it should have been written
"Contemned [i.e. boz: beit waw zayyin, i.e. the second, sixth,
and seventh days of the festival], they would not contemn
him," i.e. that they do not want the second, sixth, and seventh,
which is the substance of Samael, I should then respond:
Elsewhere it is written: "For He has not despised nor abhorred
the lowliness of the poor" (Psalms 22:25), the meaning of which
alludes to the fact that Israel does not wish to forgo love
because of the illumination that is in the libation of water on
boz (the second, sixth, and seventh days of the festival), which
is the substance of Samael, in which the evil forces do have a
portion. "They contemn him," does not refer to the light that is
in boz, but is understood literally, "that they contemn him."

COMMENTARY:

"Many waters cannot quench the love" (Song of Songs 8:7).

These are the waters of Hokhmah, about which it is written:
"Therefore with joy shall you draw water out of the wells of
salvation" (Isaiah 12:3). Although they are Hokhmah, they do
not quench the hasadim, which are called love. Likewise
"Neither can the floods drown it" (Song of Songs 8:7) refers to
the rivers of Apharsemon, for, although they contain the
illumination of Hokhmah, they, nevertheless, do not drown out
the love, i.e. they do not contract the hasadim. But "if a man,"
i.e. Samael, "would give all the substance of his house," i.e. all
the lights that he has, "for love" (ibid.) — that is, in exchange
for the annulment of the love, he would give us the lights of
the water libation on the days of boz [i.e. the second, sixth, and
seventh days of the festival — tr.], for the illumination of the
water on these days continually decreases, which shows that he
reduces the love, i.e. the hasadim, for Hokhmah, in which the
evil forces have a part, always decreases hasadim — it would
then follow that his illumination of Hokhmah would quench the
love, until Hokhmah remains without hasadim. And then the
illumination of Hokhmah would itself be quenched, for it is
unable to illuminate without hasadim (as above, Bereshit Aleph,
page 47), and, therefore: "he will be contemned" (ibid.). This is
not the case with the illumination of Hokhmah that Israel
receives; they do not quench the hasadim, which are the secret
of love.

893) A question remains to be asked: What about the first day
of the festival? The second, sixth, and seventh [boz] days are
considered those of the water libation, and the fifth, fourth
and third [charash] days are free of the libation of water, but
he does not mention the first day of the festival at all. The
answer is that the first day is not called either first nor one,
but simply "the fifteenth day (of the seventh month)" (Numbers

29:12). No special mention is made of it because there is
nothing special about it to mention, but the water libation is
first mentioned on the second day, and this is how it should be.
Because on this day a portion is given to the evil forces, it is
fitting that this should be on the second day, for about the
second day it was not said: It was good. (Cf. Genesis 1:6-8.)
This is why he does not mention the first day at all, but just
simply calls it the fifteenth day of the month, and the first
mention of the days of the festival per se, and the renewal of
the days, begins on the second day of the festival. And the
water is distributed on the boz days, i.e. the second, sixth, and
seventh days of the festival, and there is no libation of water
on the charash days, i.e. the fifth, fourth, and third, as we
have learned, and it all falls into place.

894) Happy is the portion of Israel, who know how to enter
the kernel of the nut; i.e. holiness is like the kernel of a nut
that is surrounded by shells, and in order to get to the kernel,
they break off these shells that surround it, and enter. What is
written subsequently? "On the eighth day you shall have a
solemn assembly" (Numbers 29:35). For after they break
through all these shells and break down a number of forces and
kill a number of serpents and a number of scorpions, which
were there for them in those mountains of darkness, until they
managed to find the place of settlement and a holy city which
is the holy Malkhut, surrounded by walls on all sides, they then
entered into her on the eighth day of solemn assembly to give
her pleasure there and to rejoice in her, and we have already
taught this matter (above, 33).

895) And the meaning of "solemn assembly" is a gathering, i.e.
Malkhut, for she is a place at which everything gathers, for she
is a receptacle for all the upper lights. "You shall have a solemn
assembly" (Numbers 29:25), i.e. you and nobody else shall have,

for the evil forces have no part of it, but it is you who rejoice with your Master, and He with you. And on this it is written: "Be glad in the Lord, and rejoice, O righteous; and shout for joy, all you who are upright in heart."

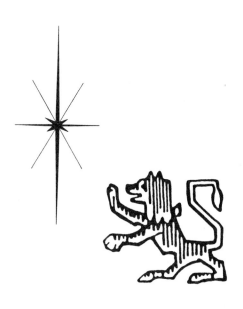

Indices

Indices

VOLUME III

— A —